ALL *for* ONE

JANETTE MARSHALL

PENGUIN BOOKS

PENGUIN BOOKS

Published by the Penguin Group
27 Wrights Lane, London W 8 5 T Z, England
Viking Penguin Inc., 40 West 23rd Street, New York, New York 10010, USA
Penguin Books Australia Ltd, Ringwood, Victoria, Australia
Penguin Books Canada Ltd, 2801 John Street, Markham, Ontario, Canada L 3 R 1 B 4
Penguin Books (NZ) Ltd, 182–190 Wairau Road, Auckland 10, New Zealand

Penguin Books Ltd, Registered Offices: Harmondsworth, Middlesex, England

First published 1990
10 9 8 7 6 5 4 3 2 1

Made and printed in Great Britain by
Cox and Wyman Ltd, Reading, Berks.

Filmset in Linotron Sabon by
Rowland Phototypesetting Ltd, Bury St Edmunds, Suffolk

CONTENTS

FOREWORD BY AUDREY EYTON 7

INTRODUCTION 9

ALL FOR ONE 13

RECIPES 25

Delicatessen Suppers
(see also Snack Suppers) 29

Drinks 37

Fish 39

Game and Poultry 51

Meat 59

Pasta 65

Salads and Salad Meals 71

Salades Tièdes
(or Warm Salads) 83

Snack Suppers
(and all about Pizza) 91

Soups 101

Mainly Vegetarian 105

Fruit Salads, Other Puddings
(and Quick Comforters) 113

Left-overs 125

INDEX 129

FOREWORD

As one of the heralds of the high-fibre revolution early in the 1980s, I was recently asked by a journalist to forecast the next big swing in eating habits. That was easy. The evidence is everywhere around us that we are entering the age of the caring food-consumer.

After decades of mindless munching we are at last beginning to ask questions about how our vegetables are grown and – much more important, in my view – in what state of misery the wretched creatures who provide our animal foods have existed.

For the onset of my own age of enlightenment I am totally indebted to the younger generation. When first my niece and her boyfriend, then the boy next door, and then my own son gave up eating meat, I decided the time had come to look into these questions which so concerned them, of how we keep and kill farm animals.

Fear not, I am not about to regale you with the dreadful details of what I discovered. Suffice it to say that previous centuries of bull-baiting and cock-fighting look positively kind-hearted compared with our present age of factory farming.

But the tide is beginning to turn. The middle-aged are turning away from foods like pork and battery eggs out of concern for cholesterol, chemicals and other dangers which threaten their health. The young (how very much nicer they are than us!) are refusing the same foods out of concern for the pigs and hens forced to endure barbaric close-confinement systems. For whichever reason, we are becoming more caring consumers. As such, we rightly require more caring cookery writers – like Janette Marshall.

No recent convert to current food concerns, Janette was strongly opposed to modern intensive farming methods many years before most of us gave them a thought, and her concern shines through in the pages of this book. Without putting us to any extra trouble she shows us how to make simple and delicious meals which also happen to be good for us. Her recipes guide us naturally towards vegetable oils rather than cholesterol-raising animal fats, to an emphasis on fish, which is so much better for health (and weight) than meat. She tempts us to eat more fresh vegetables with her clever salads.

This is a most original and exciting book on cooking-for-one, for a welcome new era of good eating.

AUDREY EYTON

INTRODUCTION

You have probably looked twice at the title of this book, thinking it sounds familiar but not quite right. Well, it will be familiar because it is taken from the motto of those three larger-than-life creations of Alexandre Dumas – the Three Musketeers.

'One for all and all for one' was the cry of this merry band and it seems appropriate to think of them when considering a cookbook that caters for the occasions when you will be eating alone because they were so adept at adjusting to their individual and joint needs and adventures. When together they shared meals, experiences and an infectious *joie de vivre*, but sometimes of course they also found themselves at separate tables, when things were 'all for one'.

This book is for the days on which you find yourself cooking, or more simply preparing, food for one. There are recipes and there are suggestions for no-cook foods.

You will find ideas for quick snacks and for light suppers alongside more complicated dishes. In this way I hope that you will find something to suit every occasion.

I would really like you to view the book as sections of ideas. I don't think any recipe, like any branch of science, is absolute. The recipes included here are simply possibilities that you can adapt; they are based on my experiences with ingredients that go together, but all the time you remain free to alter them and adapt them to your own tastes and needs. Of course I hope your tastes will be reflected in many of the dishes in *All for One*.

I also want to persuade you with the suggestions and recipes contained in *All for One* that you can have as much fun cooking for one as you can have in cooking for family and friends. When you have only yourself to please it should be possible to enjoy yourself, whatever your age or your ability in the kitchen.

I have also departed from the normal approach of cookbooks that cater for one or two portions because most of them emphasize the use of the cheapest cuts of meat, which are often the fattiest. Meat can also be problematic because of modern methods of animal husbandry. For this reason I use organically produced meat, free-range poultry and game (you will also see that I stipulate free-range eggs, this is something I have always done).

Organically produced meat usually tastes better and cooks better. It does not contain drug residues. The livestock animals should have been cared for humanely. This will sound contradictory to vegetarian readers, but it is important for meat eaters and 'demi-vegetarians' who occasionally eat meat and fish. (Any disgruntled vegetarians might like to refer to my book *Fast Food for Vegetarians* also published by Penguin.)

There are lots of fish recipes here and it's good to know that latest scientific research has revealed how good fish is for beating heart disease because of the special properties of fish oils.

After that slight digression you will see why I think some cookbooks in the past have made false economies by encouraging the use of cheap non-nutritious foods. Nevertheless, there are many low-cost nutritious ingredients such as oily fish (herring, mackerel), offal, beans and pulses.

While *All for One* is not outrageously extravagant, I think there should be a more celebratory attitude to cooking for oneself. Obviously not every night is party night, but I think that 'single eaters' are far more willing to experiment and to try new or exotic ingredients and dishes than recipe books in the past have given credit or scope for. Given the right inspiration, I am sure the solo cook would be willing to spend more time in the kitchen. For these reasons, you won't find a hundred and one things to do with a pound of mince in *All for One*. Instead you will find lots of ideas – not necessarily original, because there are very few truly original recipes, and like other cooks I have been influenced by peers and predecessors – and, hopefully, delicious combinations of ingredients that you have not previously thought of.

You will also see that I make reference to the 'health status' of various foods and often give suggestions for lower-fat or lower-sugar variations. This is because I have had a long-term interest in diet and health, and ten years' experience of writing on these subjects. So perhaps you might also pick up a few new healthy habits, as well as enjoying new dishes and adding variety to your table. I hope so.

ALL *for* ONE

I'd like you to watch a video with me. Not a cookery video, but a video which launched a new range of microwave ready-meals for one.

After the hype about the care, attention and money spent on devising a range of popular ethnic recipe dishes at a calorie cost of not more than 300 a meal the video showed people eating them, and this in particular is what I would like to show you.

Enter an attractive, slim, blonde model to a pristine kitchen studio set. She takes a meal from a drawer, peels off the lid and pops the container back into the sleeve which, says the video voice-over, 'acts as a handy splashguard'. She puts the meal into the microwave, presses the relevant buttons and the meal cooks for three minutes (fascinating viewing so far . . . are you still with me?).

She takes the meal from the oven, removes the sleeve and dishes it out on to a plate already containing a salad garnish (I suppose she has spent the three minutes tossing this together, or perhaps she has opened a packet of ready-washed salad). She crosses the kitchen to a small pine table laid with a knife and fork, a glass and an individual bottle of sparkling mineral water, and eats the meal.

Exit attractive model.

Enter dark-haired girl in school uniform. Age? Around thirteen. The girl now repeats the procedure that her mother (?) has just gone through (pity they missed each other) and eats her single-portion microwave meal – minus the side salad.

Exit schoolgirl.

Enter very ordinary-looking man in a cardigan. Can he really be the partner of the model? Perhaps he's the lodger, or the gardener. He then goes through the same procedure – minus the side salad – and eats the meal direct from the container in which it was cooked, accompanied by a glass of wine (*not* drunk from a bottle).

Finis.

Now why have I shown you this video? Because these solo diners were treating their home as a petrol station, just pulling up in front of the microwave to refuel. Certainly it's a shame they missed each other and didn't share the enjoyment and sociability of preparing and cooking a meal from fresh ingredients. Or perhaps I wanted to imply that convenience foods are bad for you?

Eating alone as the norm

No, I'm not saying there is no place in a busy modern lifestyle for ready-prepared meals. Of course there is, provided they are produced, stored and cooked carefully to avoid problems of food poisoning and infection.

The trouble is that convenience foods may not always be prepared with your nutritional welfare in mind. While it's OK to eat them occasionally it might not be a good idea to eat them too regularly, though as busy people we probably all use them from time to time.

But the poignancy of the video, and the point I want to make, is that this may now be the norm. It is very common, even within shared households, for everyone to be living their own lives, coming and going at different times, making it unlikely that most meals are now eaten in the company of others.

There are today an increasing number of single households, more working women and less time spent in the home – and especially in the kitchen. Consequently the use of ready meals is increasing – the value of the market rose from £400 million in 1985 to £600 million in 1988, and ownership of microwave ovens to re-heat convenience foods is also increasing. It's estimated that four out of ten homes have them and by 1992 this will be six out of ten. Britain is fifth in the league of microwave ownership, after America, Canada, Japan and Australia.

The single-eater syndrome

So what? So, this means that an increasing number of people are likely to fall into what might be called the single-eater syndrome. Don't worry, it's not a major new diet-related disease of Western civilization, it's the tendency of single eaters not to fuss with meals. When you are on your own you tend not to bother to prepare a meal – 'It's not worth it just for me.' Instead you snack on what's in the fridge or biscuit tin. Even if we do not live alone we may still fall into this trap when others in the household are working late, or are away from home, or when their mealtimes don't coincide with ours.

Again, I'm not saying that this is a bad way of eating. Snacking, or 'grazing' as it has been termed in America, can be as nutritious as well-planned meals – certainly smaller, lighter meals are better than large, heavy ones. The trouble is, it seems to me, that it's unlikely that most of us when left on our own do snack in a slimming or nutritious way.

Look after number one

Now, I know you don't want a lecture on the need to look after yourself and I'm sure you have worked out that although you might be living or regularly eating alone you still need to make sure your diet is a healthy one, but you might find that:

- you enjoy your food more
- you make better choices, and
- you feel better

if you start treating yourself as a guest at your own table, rather than thinking, 'This will do – it's *only* for me.'

Sometimes we spoil our guests, and so we can occasionally indulge ourselves, although eating alone should not be an excuse for over-eating whether as a means of seeking solace or because there is no one to watch us being piggy.

Sometimes we ask our guests to take us as they find us and to join in with the ordinary everyday meals and conventions – although we do make that little bit of extra effort if there is a visitor in our midst. Perhaps we lay the table a little more attractively, set it with flowers, and take the time to relax over our meal.

Taking time over meals also means that you chew food thoroughly and that you register more efficiently when you have had enough. Cutting out those second helpings can have a dramatic effect on wandering waistlines in a very short time. But the main reason for relaxing over meals is that you avoid stress.

Sitting down to your meals (don't wander around eating if you are alone) *without* your troubles is a good rule. Eating under stress will inhibit digestion and prevent the absorption of all the nutrients you need from your food. Why is this particularly relevant to single eaters? Being alone for a short or a long time makes it easier in some ways to get things out of proportion, to worry and to be susceptible to stress. Having someone around to talk to or to laugh with reduces stress.

Healthy eating for one

At this point it might be appropriate to talk a little bit about the basic principles of healthy eating, which apply just as much to you if you are looking after yourself as they do to those with responsibilities for looking after the diet of others. (Just skip this section if you are confident that you have grasped the basics of healthy eating and are already putting them into practice – or skim through it to see if there's anything new to discover or to update your knowledge.)

The main points to remember are to:

- limit the amount and type of fat you eat
- limit the amount of sugar you eat
- limit the amount of salt you eat,

and to:

- replace the decreasing contribution of fats and sugars with calories from complex carbohydrate foods such as fruit and vegetables, cereals (wholemeal bread, brown rice and other grains) and pulses.

If you would like more detail . . .

FAT

In practical terms this means recognizing foods that are high in fat, especially saturated fat, and eating only small or moderate amounts of them. The experts say we shouldn't eat more than 100g or 3½ oz of fat a day, and not more than a third of that should be saturated.

The benefit of limiting fat intake is a reduction in the risk of heart disease, and of becoming overweight which is in itself undesirable and also increases the likelihood of other health problems.

The types of fatty foods you should be wary of are fatty meat, hard and cream cheeses and other full-fat and medium-fat cheeses, full-fat milk, cream, cakes, pastries, pies and biscuits, fried foods, butter and other spreads.

You do need some fat intake because fats contain essential substances that your body can't make and without which you would become ill. These substances are found in fish oils and in polyunsaturated fats, which is why these have become – to use an Americanism – 'heart healthy' foods.

What to spread on your bread

If you would like further clarification of the common confusion over butter and other spreads, read on.

Butter is mainly saturated fat which is why it can be left out of your diet – although it would be a shame to go without it completely because there are some instances where the flavour is irreplaceable.

Margarines can be made from animal, vegetable and fish oils. Some are high in polyunsaturates and these are the ones experts are still recommending despite controversy about cancer risks from polyunsaturates, for everyday spreading – thinly – on your bread. I say 'thinly' because they are still fats, and they are no lower in calories than butter.

The polyunsaturates controversy centres on harmful free-radicals which are produced when polyunsaturates break down (during digestion). Unrefined vegetable oils and some margarines contain vitamin E which 'mops up' free-radicals. However, those who eat a lot of polyunsaturates might be wise to increase their intake of vitamins A, C and E.

Butter and margarine contain the same number of calories, weight for weight. Only low-fat spreads have fewer – they contain 40 per cent fat compared with 80 per cent for butter and margarine. Very few low-fat spreads are also high in polyunsaturates. Low-fat spreads are mainly useful for helping to control your weight, because fats are the foods containing the highest number of calories. However, they are expensive and you may prefer to learn to use less spread or enjoy your bread the continental way – without spread.

Don't forget oils

Oils such as corn, soya, sunflower, safflower, rape-seed and blended vegetable are higher in calories than butter and spreads, but, except for palm, coconut and some blends, they are also as high, or higher, in polyunsaturates. Olive oil is different: it is high in monounsaturates which it now seems may be as good for the heart as polyunsaturates, and in some ways better.

SUGAR

Just as most of us eat too much fat, so we also eat too much sugar, which is not surprising because it's natural to prefer sweet flavours to bitter ones – and because refined sugar is easy to eat.

Having been taught that sugar equals energy we tend to think of sugar as 'a good thing', but calories are all – apart from a sweet taste – you will get from sugar. It does not contain any fibre, vitamins or minerals, so nutritionally it is empty – it just clocks up the calories. In fact you don't *need* sugar because your body breaks down complex carbohydrate foods (see above) into sugars which give you energy, and in the process the body gets the nutrients and fibre it does not get from sugar.

It makes sense to replace sugar with nutritionally more satisfying foods and in the process you will be helping to maintain, or lose, weight and protect your teeth against caries. Eating too much sugar may also be linked with maturity-onset diabetes and (although this is a controversial area) with other health problems too.

If you need to reduce your sugar intake, start with the 'visible sugar' added to drinks, cereals and fruit and then cut down on confectionery, patisserie, cakes, biscuits and sugary processed foods and drinks, from breakfast cereals in the morning through to desserts in the evening. Perhaps a 'puddings at weekends only' rule, or confectionery just on certain days, might be helpful. Overall you are aiming for not more than 2 oz or around 50g of sugar a day, including the sugar hidden in ready-prepared foods.

FIBRE

Since the *F-Plan diet* we have all become aware of the importance of enough fibre in our diet to keep us both slim and generally in better health. One very easy way to ensure a healthy diet is to adopt as a long-term goal the replacement of sugary and fatty foods with high-fibre ones.

As a general practice, choose wholemeal and other whole grain breads instead of white (of course you don't have to *give up* crusty white French bread!), and wholemeal pasta instead of white. You don't have to become vegetarian, but you will benefit by increasing the amount of beans, pulses, chickpeas, lentils and so on that you eat by including them in meat dishes; and indeed some meat meals could be replaced by vegetarian wholefood meals or ethnic dishes from India, China, Mexico, the Middle East and Mediterranean countries where pulses are used as an important source of protein.

Eating a high-fibre breakfast cereal is a convenient way of ensuring a good proportion of the 30g of fibre we are recommended to aim for each day. It doesn't have to be bran-based – in fact sugar and fat are often used to make the bran palatable. One based on whole grains, such as muesli, Shredded Wheat or Weetabix, is fine. Sprinkling with raw bran is not necessary, and can also interfere with your mineral absorption as substances in bran may bind with them and make them unavailable to you.

The 'soluble' fibre in oats, oatbran and beans (wheat bran is 'insoluble') is also important because if you eat enough (and no scientists will say *exactly* how much is enough – perhaps 2–3 oz oats a day) it can lower cholesterol levels.

ORGANIC FOOD

Why organic? After taking the trouble to alter your diet and learn about the principles of healthier eating (and a healthier lifestyle including exercise and proper relaxation) you want to know that the food you are buying meets the standards you have set yourself.

Organic food is produced by a sustainable system of agriculture that supports the environment and does not result in the food you eat containing chemical and drug residues from modern farming techniques. All the staple foods – meat and veg, fruit, cereals, pulses and dairy produce, vegetable oils and in addition even wine and coffee are produced organically.

Fortunately, you no longer have to dig your own allotment because most major multiples have sprouted organic produce along with their other 'green' merchandise, but as suppliers are patchy it's worth finding more than one stockist in your area.

Slimming

You will have noticed that I have made references to slimming and maintaining your correct weight in this discussion of the basics of a good diet. Really there is no need to think about counting calories, or about dieting, if you take the long-term approach to a well-balanced diet outlined above.

By avoiding fatty and sugary foods and eating instead more complex carbohydrate foods on a regular daily basis you should in time find your correct weight and maintain it. Of course you also need to take regular exercise, learn to relax, and cope with – or avoid – stress so that you are not prone to 'binge eating' or seeking comfort in food by over-eating.

Quick cooking for one

Cooking for one is no different from cooking for a hundred, except for quantities. Your aim is still the same: delicious, fresh and well-cooked food. However, there are some items that you might find especially helpful in your *batterie de cuisine*.

For example, a combination microwave oven. Because such an oven can supply both convection and microwave heat, the speed of microwave cooking can be combined with the advantages of convection heat in browning the food.

When you are cooking for one it is tempting to think that it is not worth heating the oven for one baked potato, for example, although, of course, it is! Baking a potato in a combination oven takes far less time – around twenty minutes – and it has a brown, crispy skin just like a potato cooked in a conventional oven.

A combination oven should save you money because you will use less electricity. Microwave cooking is energy-saving: microwave ovens are 40 per cent efficient compared with 14 per cent for electric ovens and only 7 per cent for gas (efficiency is the ratio of energy utilized to energy actually given out by the appliance). Baking in a conventional oven uses nearly 1 kilowatt per hour compared with 0.17 in a microwave oven.

A pressure cooker is another invaluable investment for cooking single portions or meals. It will cut the cooking time by half and it means you can cook casseroles and other traditionally 'long cook' items on the hob without the expense of heating the oven. It seems astonishing but a pressure cooker produces a meal in two-thirds of the time it would take to cook it in the oven, and for less than the cost of conventional cooking.

From a nutritional point of view, microwave ovens and pressure cookers also retain more nutrients (vitamins and minerals) in the food because it is cooked more quickly. You can also cook food without adding water, in the case of the microwave, or without the food coming into contact with water, in the case of the pressure cooker. This prevents vitamins and minerals leaching out during cooking and being thrown away with the cooking water.

I used a Brother Hi-Speed Combination microwave oven when devising recipes for *All for One*. It offers three separate cooking methods: high-speed, turbo and microwave. High-speed cooking uses simultaneously microwave energy and recirculating hot air. There is no need to pre-heat and you obtain the browned results of conventional cooking in a fraction of the time. Turbo cooking cooks the food by forcing hot air over heated electric elements and then over the food. Turbo cooking can be done with the turntable or without it; if you don't use it you have the corners of the oven to fit in more items.

I also used a Tefal stainless-steel 2.7 litre pressure cooker suitable for all types of hobs, including Aga hotplates and ceramic hobs. This size is ideal when cooking in single portions, yet at the same time it was large enough to allow me to make marmalade!

Equipping oneself . . .

I recommend a stainless-steel pressure cooker (and saucepans) because, unlike aluminium, it does not react with food – such a reaction can result in minute amounts of aluminium being deposited in whatever you are cooking. Stainless steel utensils are also longer-lasting.

Other equipment you need will simply be that of a standard kitchen, although you might prefer a greater selection of smaller pots, pans and dishes. If you enjoy cooking and intend to prepare some sophisticated dishes it is worth investing in the correct equipment so that you are not handicapped, or disappointed, by a lack of the right tools for the job. On the other hand, if you intend to be a minimalist cook then there is not much point in investing in items you are not going to use – unless you mean to invite friends who are cooks to work in your kitchen.

As a very brief guide, especially for those starting from scratch, you might find the following list useful: balloon whisk, basins, blender (or liquidizer/food processor/mixer), bread board and knife, can-opener, chopping boards (separate ones for meat, please, to ensure good food hygiene. Separate sides of another for fruit and veg to ensure no garlic-flavoured fruit salads), stainless-steel colander, fruit juicer/squeezer, garlic press, grater, knives (vegetable knife, small cook's knife, parer, large cook's knife, grapefruit knife), masher, measuring jug, mixing bowl, pestle and mortar (as useful as it is aesthetically pleasing), rolling-pin, salad bowl, saucepans (if you want only one, the best is a marmite with an omelette pan on top which doubles as a lid – useful both on the hob and in the oven), scales, scissors, sieve, spatula, spoons (or spoon measure), steamer, terrine/bread tin, timer (if not on cooker/microwave), vacuum flask, water filter, wok.

A small freezer is very useful for avoiding waste when you cook too much, or receive last minute invites *after* cooking or simply *have* to buy food in larger (pre-packed) quantities than you have an immediate need for.

RECIPES

The recipes have been designed so that the key ingredients are picked out in SMALL CAPITAL LETTERS. This will give you an idea, at a quick glance, of whether a recipe will suit your particular taste, and whether you have the ingredients in the fridge or store-cupboard. SMALL CAPITAL LETTERS have *not* been used for items you will almost certainly have 'in stock' – salt, pepper and olive oil, for example.

However, the ingredients listed are not absolute. You can always substitute similar items or use the basis of the recipe as a starting-point for creating your own dish.

Even though you have skimmed through the ingredients, please read the whole recipe before you begin to assemble the ingredients and start preparation and cooking.

Delicatessen Suppers

PASTRAMI ON RYE

There are lots of different types of RYE BREAD. A light colour indicates that the flour is quite refined (as in white bread) and the flavour will be mild. Rye may employ yeast as the raising agent or be a sourdough bread using a sourdough starter to make the mixture rise – the nicest example of the latter is *Pain Poîlane* from Paris, sold in selected London cheese and wine shops.

Darker rye breads made from the wholemeal equivalent of rye flour will be denser in texture – and tastier; some may contain whole grains of sprouted or malted rye, in pumpernickel style. If you are buying a whole loaf the left-over will freeze satisfactorily, if well wrapped.

Lightly SPREAD with unsalted BUTTER, or a high-in-polyunsaturates margarine, or a low-fat spread, depending on where you are in the cholesterol stakes. Pile slices high with thinly sliced PASTRAMI (2–4 oz/50–100g, depending on how hungry you are). Garnish with HORSERADISH SAUCE on the side of the plate, plenty of pickled GHERKINS and either a green side SALAD or COLESLAW.

BLT – BACON, LETTUCE
AND TOMATO SANDWICH

Grill a couple of rashers of BACON, smoked back if you like it full of flavour, or green if you prefer it milder, and pat off excess fat with kitchen paper. I use organically produced bacon because it tastes superior, has a better texture and contains less sodium nitrite and sodium nitrate (E250, E251), somewhat problematic food additives. Bacon has to contain saltpetre (E251, E252) without which it would be salt pork. Look out for 'traditional cure' or 'dry cure' bacons in supermarkets. They are pre-packed (a disadvantage when shopping for one), but they are tastier and in packs of 6–8 rashers. Surplus freezes well.

Toast some wholemeal BREAD on one side, then fill the sandwich with the bacon, crispy LETTUCE, slices of ripe, juicy TOMATO and some low-calorie MAYONNAISE. Pile some low- or reduced-fat crisps on the side of the plate.

BAGELS

These delicious golden-brown bread rolls with a hole in the middle are made of a simple white-flour dough and are deep fried, but they are not fatty like doughnuts (about 150 calories each compared with 130 for a bap or bread roll). The most famous bagels are spread with CREAM CHEESE and topped with SMOKED SALMON. For a 'healthier' version, use a lower-fat curd cheese, or a quark flavoured with chopped chives or other herbs, then top with slices of smoked salmon. Some delicatessens sell 'sandwich pieces' (offcuts) of smoked salmon – just make sure there is not too much dark-brown meat or pieces of skin before you buy. If you are tired of smoked salmon (some people are!) try fresher and less salty gravad lax (pronounced *grav-lax*) – salmon marinated with dill, seasoning and sugar – with your bagels.

TURKISH BAGELS

A delightful waterside restaurant which cookery writer Jill Tilsley-Benham introduced me to: Kanlica Körfez on the Asian side of the Bosporus in Istanbul, makes the most delicious 'butter' which is wonderful as a bagel topping. It makes use of the classic, if ubiquitous, Turkish aubergine salad called *patlikan* (Turkish for aubergine) *salata*.

Grill a small AUBERGINE under a hot grill, or turn it in a gas flame. The skin will char, but this is OK. When cooked, scrape off the charred skin and put the flesh in a blender with 2 oz/50g unsalted BUTTER, a clove of crushed GARLIC, a tablespoonful of LEMON JUICE and some very finely chopped fresh TARRAGON. Blend to a smooth, light purée.

CHÈVRE ON TOAST

Doubly unfortunate in being a culinary cliché and high in calories, but still delicious, so don't deny yourself! Take thin slices from a GOAT'S CHEESE log – normal size or miniature cocktail size – or slices of *reblochon* with the rind cut away. Toast one side of your favourite BREAD (mine varies between *Pain Poîlane*, a sourdough rye bread, Vogel, well-made wholemeal, Italian, and French crusty white) and then spread the untoasted side with GARLIC BUTTER. Top with the cheese slices and lightly toast under the grill.

Alternatively, spread ready-made French Toasts from the deli with garlic butter and top with cheese before toasting lightly.

CHINESE PRAWN TOAST

Mash 2 oz/50g shelled, defrosted North Atlantic PRAWNS. (If you don't mind, a minor digression on prawns: try not to use warm-water or 'tropical' prawns because while they appear to be a cheaper bargain they are generally tough, chewy and tasteless. If you cook with them they shrivel to nothing and remain hard.)

Back to the mashed prawns: add a small amount of LEMON JUICE and a little SZECHUAN PEPPER or Chinese five-spice mix if you have it. Cut the crusts off two thin slices of wholemeal BREAD and toast one side of each under the grill. Spread the untoasted sides of the bread with the prawns and – this is optional – gently press some SESAME SEEDS on top. Place under the grill to heat through and lightly brown the seeds.

RICOTTA AND SPINACH PARCELS

Defrost about 4 oz/100g FILO PASTRY or strudel leaves and lay them out flat. Defrost 2 oz/50g frozen SPINACH and mix with 5 oz/150g RICOTTA CHEESE. Season, and stir in about 1 oz/25g PINE KERNELS. Place the mixture in strips on the pastry and roll up into small parcels. Brush with ¼ oz/7g melted unsalted BUTTER and bake for about 12 minutes at 375°F/190°C/Gas 5.

OMELETTE AUX TRUFFES

Truffle omelette is a speciality of the truffle-producing regions of France and Spain. Lightly beat a couple of free-range EGGS and season with sea salt and a little freshly ground black pepper. Cut some slivers of TRUFFLE and lightly cook them in a mixture of ½ oz/15g melted unsalted BUTTER and half a table-spoon of olive oil in your omelette pan. Then pour in the beaten eggs and cook the omelette. Freshly chopped chives are a good addition. Enjoy with warm, crusty French bread . . . Some people (not me) like this with a glass of sweet white wine.

SHIRRED EGGS AND SMOKED SALMON

A variation on the theme of scrambled eggs and smoked salmon. Beat together two free-range EGGS and stir in a table-spoonful of CREAM or skimmed milk and a pinch of GROUND CORIANDER. Melt a knob of unsalted BUTTER in a pan, or a mixture of butter and olive oil, and pour in the beaten eggs. Using a wooden spatula, draw the eggs across the pan until lightly set. By working quickly you will get flakes of egg, not scrambled egg. Spoon on to a plate and top with slivers of SMOKED SALMON (about 1 oz/25g) and a few fresh CORIANDER LEAVES. Season with freshly ground black pepper and eat with toasted *ciabatta* (Italian bread made with olive oil).

PARMA PARCELS WITH HUMMUS

Thin slices of PARMA HAM wrapped around home-made hummus is delicious, especially when eaten with slices of juicy, fragrant melon and light Italian bread. To make the hummus, simply blend the following in a food processor: half a can (14 oz/400g) cooked CHICKPEAS, a rounded tablespoon of light TAHINI, one fat clove of crushed GARLIC, the juice of half a LEMON, 3 oz/75g low-fat soft white cheese such as QUIRK (or Greek yoghurt), a tablespoonful of olive oil, and freshly ground black pepper.

SMOKED MACKEREL PÂTÉ

Flake a fillet of SMOKED MACKEREL from the skin, removing any bones as you do so. Beat with 4 oz/100g COTTAGE CHEESE or quark (low-fat soft white cheese), a teaspoonful of LEMON JUICE, and a little GROUND MACE and black pepper.

SMOKED SALMON PÂTÉ

Blend in a food processor 4 oz/100g SMOKED SALMON 'sandwich pieces' (offcuts), 3 oz/75g CURD CHEESE, one tablespoonful of olive oil, two teaspoons of LEMON JUICE, and freshly ground black PEPPER.

CHICKEN LIVER PÂTÉ

Hard-boil a free-range EGG, then drain, cool, shell and finely dice it. Finely dice an ONION, crush a clove of GARLIC and sweat both in a pan with a little olive oil. Chop about 4 oz/100g CHICKEN LIVERS, add to the onion and garlic and cook for about 3 minutes, leaving the liver pink inside. Remove from the heat and stir in the chopped egg. Add about ½ oz/15g softened unsalted BUTTER and season with freshly ground black PEPPER and GROUND MACE. Place in a ramekin in the fridge to set. (If you have stopped cooking chicken products lightly since reports of an increased incidence of salmonella, then wait until you are again confident before trying the recipe rather than spoil the dish by overcooking the liver.)

WALNUT AND ANCHOVY PÂTÉ

A rich pâté that is delicious on toast, crisp rolls or crispbread. It keeps well in the fridge for about ten days if covered. Sweat a diced ONION in the microwave or a covered pan until soft. Remove from the heat and place in a liquidizer or food processor with a couple of teaspoons of ANCHOVY PURÉE and a small drained can of ANCHOVIES patted with kitchen paper to remove excess oil. Add about 2 oz/50g each of WALNUT PIECES and wholemeal BREADCRUMBS and blend to the consistency you prefer for pâté, fine or coarse. If you like, you can stir in some low-fat soft white cheese such as QUARK to make the pâté go further or to give a milder flavour.

STILTON AND WALNUT PÂTÉ

This is a variation of the above, substituting 4 oz/100g blue STILTON CHEESE for the anchovies and anchovy purée.

LENTILS AND CHORIZO

A typical *tapas* dish of lentils and Spanish sausage, but more than an accompaniment to an aperitif: served alongside beans, or perhaps wild mushrooms with peppers, this makes a meal in itself. It's also quite healthy in that you are extending meat by the use of lentils (which are one of the few quickly cooked pulses). Use WHOLE GREEN LENTILS. Pick them over to remove any stones or grit, then wash well in two or three changes of water. Put in a saucepan with about twice the volume of good VEGETABLE or MEAT STOCK and bring to the boil. Reduce heat and simmer for about 10 minutes, then slice up a spicy CHORIZO SAUSAGE and add to the lentils. Cook with the lid on for a further 15 minutes, topping up with stock if necessary, and it's ready to serve. This also makes a tasty cold salad dish.

BROAD BEANS WITH HAM

Broad beans are one of my favourite vegetables. Small, sweet young BROAD BEANS are delicious just shelled and simply steamed, but if they are not in season you will have to use frozen ones. Somehow they taste even better with ham, which can be chopped and mixed with them, or, if it's a delicious Spanish *JAMÓN SERRANO*, for example, served in slices alongside the beans with some crusty *ciabatta*.

IF TIME IS SHORT . . .

If you've had to shop in a hurry you cannot always ensure that the cheese is perfectly matured or that the wine has been gradually reaching room temperature during the day. There may not be a convenient good-quality Indian takeaway for poppodums on your way home from work, or you may have decided to do a breaded dish but don't want to buy commercial dry bread-crumbs because of the colourings they contain. Here are a few handy hints that seem to fit delicatessen-type buys:

- If the Brie or Camembert is not as ripe as you would like or is still cold from the chiller or fridge, and you need to eat *now*, you can 'ripen' it by microwaving for about 10–15 seconds on Full power, then leave it to stand for 5 minutes.
- You can *chambrer* wine in a similar way. Remove metal foils and put the bottle in the microwave on Full power for 30 seconds. Let it stand for 5 minutes.
- Poppodums can also be cooked quickly in the microwave. Three will cook on Full power in about 1–1½ minutes. Then leave them for a minute to crisp.
- The microwave will also produce dry breadcrumbs for coating. Put a couple of slices of bread on a plate and cook on High for 1½–2 minutes. Leave them for a couple of minutes and then crumb the bread in a food processor.

Drinks

LIME PRESSÉ

Squeeze the juice from a LIME and add a teaspoonful of ICING SUGAR or clear honey. Place in a glass over ice cubes and splash on SPARKLING MINERAL WATER.

MANGO AND LIME

Peel a MANGO, then cut the flesh from the stone and put half into the liquidizer. Add the juice of a LIME and a tumblerful of English APPLE JUICE. Whizz . . . and drink.

MELON ZINGER

Take half an OGEN or CHARENTAIS MELON and purée the flesh. Chill the resultant juice until you are ready to drink it. Garnish with fresh MINT LEAVES.

This is also nice mixed with fresh orange juice.

PINK GRAPEFRUIT PASSION JUICE

One of my favourite fruit-juice cocktails is a mixture of the juice of a PINK GRAPEFRUIT and the strained juice of two PASSION FRUIT, diluted with SPARKLING MINERAL WATER.

STRAWBERRY SLING

Whizz in the liquidizer about 4 oz/100g fresh, ripe (not squashy), washed and hulled STRAWBERRIES with one teaspoonful of LEMON JUICE, one tablespoonful of GRENADINE SYRUP, and either BUTTERMILK or thin natural yoghurt to taste (around ¼ pint/150ml).

BANANA FRUIT COCKTAIL

Lightly mash a small ripe BANANA and put into the liquidizer. Add from the fridge 4 oz/100g NATURAL YOGHURT (individual yoghurt pots are usually 125g or 150g) and ¼ pint/150ml unsweetened ORANGE JUICE. Blend until frothy. Pour on to ice if you like, and drink at once.

Fish

Salmon fishcakes

Fresh salmon is most delicious, but if you can't bring yourself to use even the tail end of this gourmet fish for fishcakes then use canned salmon. First peel a couple of medium-sized floury POTATOES and cut them into small pieces so that they boil quickly. Drain, and mash or liquidize half the potatoes with a little SKIMMED MILK and a dessertspoonful of MAYONNAISE; leave the rest roughly diced (if that's not too much of a contradiction!). Cook one SALMON STEAK of about 4 oz/100g *en papillote* (in a greaseproof paper pouch) for about 2 minutes in the microwave on Full power (check oven manufacturer's instructions). Flake the fish from the skin and bones and mix with all the potato and a tablespoonful of freshly chopped HERBS: for example, parsley, chives, or, for a Scandinavian flavour, dill. Season to taste with sea salt and black pepper, divide up the mixture and mould into fishcake shapes by patting in toasted BREADCRUMBS (*not* the brilliant orange shop-bought variety, please!) on a flat surface. Grill or fry. Squeeze some fresh LEMON JUICE over the fishcakes and a little freshly ground black pepper.

Smoked fish platter

Often served as a starter, but really a meal in itself. Select from old favourites such as SMOKED SALMON, freshly SMOKED EEL and MUSSELS, with perhaps a little SMOKED MACKEREL if you can find some that has not been dyed bright orange or kept in a sweaty polythene pack. For a treat, add thin slices of SMOKED TUNA ROE and some home-made TARAMOSALATA or a couple of slivers of SMOKED COD'S ROE (again, if you can obtain any that is not bright red from the addition of dye). Serve with whole-meal or whole-grain BREAD or toast, wedges of LEMON, HORSERADISH SAUCE and a glass of Chablis or Gewürztraminer. Scandinavian dill and mustard sauce also makes a good accompaniment.

SMOKED TROUT VOL-AU-VENTS

Bake some ready-made vol-au-vent cases (unless you have time to make them yourself) and when they are cool enough to handle, fill them with a SMOKED TROUT fillet liquidized (or mixed with a fork for a rougher texture) with freshly grated MACE, LEMON JUICE and four tablespoons of QUARK or strained Greek yoghurt. Stir in some freshly chopped PARSLEY or dill.

SALMON STEAKS OR CUTLETS ON CUCUMBER SAUCE

Grilled salmon is an instant gourmet meal (for far less than the price of top-quality beef fillet and with all sorts of health benefits from the fish oils). Grill a 4 oz/100g SALMON STEAK or cutlet (salmon is very filling) for 6 minutes, turning once, and make an instant no-cook sauce while it grills. Simply liquidize half a small cucumber with 2 oz/50g QUARK, *fromage frais* or other low-fat soft white cheese, a teaspoonful of WINE VINEGAR and seasoning. Place the salmon on a puddle of the sauce, if you like it that way, or offer it to yourself separately! This dish goes well with salad or new potatoes such as La Ratte (also called cornichon).

HALIBUT ON TOMATO SAUCE

Halibut is a fine and delicate fish, unlike many other white fish which are cut into fish steaks. Grill a 5 oz/150g HALIBUT STEAK which has been brushed with a little seasoned olive oil (perhaps with a variety of herbs, chillies or other spices steeped in it) and LEMON JUICE for 5 minutes, turning once. While it is cooking make an instant no-cook sauce by liquidizing two skinned TOMATOES with a tablespoonful of vinaigrette. Halibut is good with rice, or with pink fir apple potatoes whose delicate and light 'crispness' complements the texture of the fish.

SALMON TARTLET

Much easier and quicker than you would think, looking at this long explanation ... Use ready-made FILO PASTRY (also called strudel leaves) which needs no rolling out. You need three layers of pastry; conveniently, most packs of frozen filo contain two bags each of 8 oz/225g three-sheet-thick filo pastry. As one tartlet will take very little pastry, you can make something else to use up the rest – perhaps some more tartlet cases which will keep well in an airtight tin for a week, or maybe an Easy-Peasy Apple and Guava Strudel (page 120) which can be frozen, or samosas which also freeze well.

Line with pastry a lightly oiled 4"/10cm tartlet tin of 1½"/3cm depth, trim the edge, then brush with a minute amount of melted unsalted BUTTER. There's no need to fiddle around with baking beans and greaseproof paper: you can bake the tartlet as it is for 10 minutes at 375°F/190°C/Gas 5. Remove from the oven and cool. While the tartlet is cooking, poach about 3 oz/75g SALMON in a saucepan (or microwave it) in dry WHITE WINE, fish stock, vegetable or fish stock-cube, or water, with a BAY LEAF, PEPPERCORNS, CARROT and PARSLEY added to the liquid. It's easiest to use a fillet of salmon cut from the tail end and to skin it before cooking. Also boil a handful of PEAS and BROAD BEANS, frozen if necessary. Drain the fish and vegetables, mix together and place in the tartlet. Nice garnished with hard-boiled QUAIL EGGS (which take 3 minutes to cook) and a generous teaspoonful of KETA (salmon roe). Serve with a Wild Salad (page 72).

MONKFISH MASALA

A 'cheats' recipe from SHARWOOD'S using their MASALA CURRY SAUCE – tastes very good. Simply cut up about 4–5 oz/100–150g MONKFISH (or other white fish) and arrange in an ovenproof dish. Pour over the sauce and bake at 350°F/180°C/Gas 4 for 15–20 minutes. Of course if you have time to marinate the fish in the sauce for a couple of hours before cooking it will be much tastier. Serve with brown basmati RICE, or a rice mixture containing wild rice. Cooking brown rice in the pressure cooker really speeds up the operation. Put the rice in the cooker with twice its volume of cold water, bring to high pressure and cook for 6 minutes. Reduce the pressure quickly and serve.

TROUT EN CROÛTE

Defrost some PUFF PASTRY and roll it out thinly. Halve the sheet of pastry, and on one half place a skinned TROUT fillet. Slice a couple of brown champignon MUSHROOMS and lay the slices along the length of the trout. Spoon over a tablespoonful of naturally brewed SOY SAUCE. Put the second half of the pastry sheet on top, sealing the two layers together by brushing with a little milk or beaten free-range egg and pinching the edges together. Trim neatly. Place on a baking-tray and bake for 20 minutes in an oven preheated to 375°F/190°C/Gas 5. Serve with GREEN VEGETABLES and poached mushrooms.

FAST-FOOD FISH PIE

For an instant fish pie, take a frozen COD STEAK in parsley sauce and put in a pie-dish with a couple of tablespoons of frozen PEAS or sweetcorn and some additional PARSLEY. Season. Peel two medium-sized POTATOES, cut into small pieces so that they boil quickly. Drain, and mash or liquidize with a little skimmed MILK and a dessertspoonful of MAYONNAISE or salad cream. Spread the mashed potato on top of the fish (or use reconstituted instant potato if you like). Put into a preheated oven at 375°F/190°C/Gas 5 and cook for 20–25 minutes until golden brown.

SCALLOPS WITH WILD RICE

Soak a few strands of SAFFRON in a small amount of boiling water. Cook 2–3 oz/50–75g WILD RICE in boiling water for 15 minutes. While the rice is cooking, wash and slice a small LEEK. In a shallow frying-pan with a lid, sauté the leek in unsalted BUTTER for 5 minutes. Add three or four large frozen SCALLOPS to the pan, cover and leave to cook for 5 minutes. Drain the rice and add to the leek and scallops, together with the water in which the saffron has soaked (discard the saffron itself). If necessary, top up with just enough VEGETABLE or FISH STOCK to cover the rice. Simmer for 10 minutes or until the rice grains have plumped and split their skins, then serve hot.

CREOLE PRAWNS

Sweet and fiery prawns from the cooking of New Orleans – a glorious mixture of the traditional cuisine of many ethnic groups, including Portuguese, Indian, French, Spanish and African.

Shell and remove the heads from as many large, uncooked PRAWNS as you like, maybe four to six; leave these on one side while you make the sauce. Sauté a diced small ONION, half a chopped GREEN or RED PEPPER and a crushed clove of GARLIC (or more) until transparent, then add three ripe, chopped TOMATOES or the contents of a small can (7 oz/200g), a teaspoonful of raw cane (brown) SUGAR, the juice of half a LEMON and a dash or two of TABASCO (hot pepper sauce). Cook through and then add the prawns, cooking them for a further 3–4 minutes until they are opaque. Serve with RICE or a crusty bread.

BACON AND FISH KEBABS

Use whatever fish you like for these (you will need about 4–5 oz/100–150g) – white fish like COD or haddock, or a 'steaky' fish such as monkfish. Chop the fish into large cubes. Cut the rind from a couple of rashers of back BACON and flatten them on a chopping-board to stretch them. Then cut the rashers into smaller pieces and wrap a piece round each cube of fish. Thread the wrapped fish on to skewers, interspersed with slices of COURGETTE and GREEN or RED PEPPERS, whole CHERRY TOMATOES and any other suitable vegetable you may have. Sprinkle with some spikes of fresh ROSEMARY or thyme and brush lightly with olive oil and/or LEMON JUICE. Cook under a hot grill (or on a small barbecue if the weather is good) for about

10 minutes, turning the kebabs once or twice. Serve with brown
RICE.

MONKFISH PROVENÇAL
WITH POTATOES

Sauté a small, diced ONION and a clove of crushed GARLIC
in a little olive oil. Add 4–6 oz/100–175g cubed MONKFISH
and a few small scrubbed salad POTATOES such as La Ratte
(cornichon). Cook until slightly coloured. Add a small can of
TOMATOES (7 oz/200g) and some THYME, PARSLEY and
MARJORAM (or oregano) and simmer for about 15 minutes.

BRAISED TUNA

TUNA or swordfish steaks are very good when baked or
braised (and when grilled). Place the skinned and boned steak in
an ovenproof dish and top with sliced TOMATO and ONION.
Sprinkle with a tablespoonful of mixed LEMON JUICE and olive oil
and season with sea salt and freshly ground black pepper. Add a
couple of tablespoons of water and some freshly chopped PARS-
LEY and THYME, and bake in a slow oven (325°F/170°C/Gas 3) for
40 minutes.

LENTILS WITH MUSSELS

Cook some whole GREEN LENTILS, about 2–3 oz/50–75g
dry weight, in plenty of boiling water for about 20 minutes or
until tender. Drain, if the lentils have not absorbed all the water,
and marinate immediately in a salad dressing made from OLIVE
OIL, WHITE WINE VINEGAR, freshly ground black pepper and
crushed cloves of GARLIC. Let the lentils steep for at least an hour.
When you are ready to eat, prepare some fresh MUSSELS (up to 1 lb
per person, weighed in their shells). Scrub the mussels and scrape
off any barnacles, etc., pull off the byssus threads (beards) and
wash them in cold water. Discard any shells that are open. Put into
a large saucepan with a little water or white wine and bring to the

boil with a lid on the pan. Sprinkle with some chopped PARSLEY, or other herbs of your choice, as the mussels open. Cook until all the shells are open (discard any that remain closed) – this will take about 5 minutes. Serve the mussels with the lentils, which can be reheated or eaten cold.

CHILLI PRAWNS

In a mortar, crush the seeds from a couple of green CARDAMOMS and half a teaspoon of CORIANDER SEEDS to a powder. Then wash some RICE (about 2 oz/50g) and put it on to cook; the prawns will take about as long to cook as boiled or steamed brown rice which can be eaten with them. Sauté a crushed clove of GARLIC, a small diced ONION and a diced green CHILLI in a little OLIVE OIL, then add the prepared spices and a pinch of TURMERIC powder. Cook for a minute, add about 4 oz/100g PRAWNS, and then pour in the juice of half an ORANGE and a couple of roughly chopped ripe TOMATOES which will disintegrate as you cook. Continue to stir the mixture for about 10–15 minutes while the dish finishes cooking.

STUFFED SQUID

You can stuff either baby SQUID, in which case you might need two or three, or larger squid, when normally one will suffice. If starting from scratch, hold the squid by the tentacles, pull off the head and remove the insides and beak, then cut off the tentacles but don't throw them away. Pull the quills out of the body and discard the ink sacs.

To make the stuffing: chop the tentacles and put them in a frying-pan or saucepan with a couple of diced rashers of un-smoked back BACON, a tablespoonful each of LEMON JUICE and olive oil, freshly ground black pepper and a level tablespoonful of PINE KERNELS. If you just happen to have any cold cooked RICE, this can also be added. You might also like to add a chopped TOMATO for added moisture. Cook the stuffing mixture gently for about 3 minutes (longer, if the squid is to be grilled – see below), then stuff the body of the squid with it. Close the end with a wooden cocktail stick.

You then have a choice of how to complete the cooking. You can grill the squid or bake them in the oven. To bake, carefully sauté the stuffed squid until slightly brown, and then arrange in an ovenproof dish to which you can add a small amount of dry WHITE WINE or some tomato juice or vegetable stock, and a little more olive oil to prevent sticking. Season, and cook in a moderate oven (350°F/180°C/Gas 4) for 35–40 minutes. If grilling, the stuffing mixture must be cooked for a little longer – about 15 minutes. Brush the stuffed squid with olive oil, season, and grill, turning several times, for 15–20 minutes.

STEAMED SKATE

SKATE wing will usually weigh around 1 lb/450g, so ask your fishmonger for half a wing. Trim off the frilly edge. Place the fish in a steamer basket, sprinkle with some grated zest of LIME and a small amount of grated FRESH GINGER, and season lightly. Cover and steam for about 5 minutes. Serve with RICE or noodles and a GREEN VEGETABLE such as very lightly sautéd courgettes.

MOULES MARINIÈRE

Scrub and scrape clean 1 lb/450g of fresh, tightly closed MUSSELS, pulling off the byssus threads (beards) as you do so. Finely dice two or three SHALLOTS (or one small onion), crush a couple of cloves of GARLIC, and put these in a pan large enough to contain the mussels. Add a glass of dry WHITE WINE, cider, or vegetable or fish stock, and bring to the boil. Add the mussels and cook for about 10 minutes or until they are all open. (Discard any that remain closed.) Sprinkle with a handful of freshly chopped PARSLEY and transfer to a serving bowl. GARLIC BREAD is a good accompaniment.

SCALLOP OR OYSTER BROCHETTES

SCALLOPS and OYSTERS make delicious brochettes (food grilled on a skewer – for the method, see Bacon and Fish Kebabs, page 44) when wrapped in lean BACON. Sprinkle with the juice from a wedge of LEMON and with freshly ground black pepper. Eat with brown RICE and grilled PEPPERS or aubergines, ratatouille, green beans or a salad.

SCALLOPS WITH NEW VEGETABLES

Prepare four good-sized SCALLOPS (or buy them ready-to-cook or frozen). Prepare some baby CARROTS, baby LEEKS and young GREEN BEANS or peas. Bring ½ pint/300ml VEGETABLE STOCK or *court-bouillon* to simmering point in a pan. Add a squeeze of LEMON JUICE and the vegetables, and boil for 5 minutes. Lower again to simmering point, add the scallops and cook for a further 5–6 minutes. Put the scallops and vegetables on a hot serving dish and cover to keep warm. Strain about a teacupful of the cooking liquid through a sieve.

If you want to thicken the liquid you can simply purée some more vegetables. Or you may find you prefer the following *nouvelle cuisine* method of thickening sauces to the traditional *roux* base of flour and butter, which is high in calories and fat. Mix together in a saucepan a tablespoonful of CRÈME FRAÎCHE (or double cream) and the yolk of a free-range EGG. Slowly pour on to the cream and egg yolk mixture the hot liquid from the scallops and vegetables. Stir over a very low heat to thicken, then pour the sauce over the scallops and vegetables. Garnish with freshly chopped CHERVIL.

GRILLED OYSTERS

Open six OYSTERS, or ask the fishmonger to do it for you. Leave them in the deep side of the shell. Sprinkle with finely chopped SHALLOTS and freshly ground black pepper, or with chopped chives and a little lemon juice. Grill under a very fierce heat for 2–3 minutes and serve immediately.

OYSTERS MORNAY

Combinations of cheese and fish are not my particular favourites, but this is popular, so you might like it! Open six OYSTERS and remove from their shells. Clean the shells. Poach the oysters in a little dry WHITE WINE for 2–3 minutes, replace them in the shells and spoon over a small quantity of White Sauce (see below) to which you have added 1 oz/25g grated GRUYÈRE CHEESE. Brown under a very hot grill and eat at once with a squeeze of LEMON JUICE.

I prefer Oysters *à l'Américaine* – topped with a sauce of WHITE WINE, crushed GARLIC, sliced SHALLOTS and diced fresh TOMATOES.

WHITE SAUCE

Stir together in a pan half a tablespoon each of plain FLOUR and either soft vegetable MARGARINE, unsalted butter or vegetable oil to make a *roux* (thick paste). Cook gently for one minute, then slowly add about ⅓ pint/180ml SKIMMED MILK, stirring all the time, to make a smooth white sauce. Season.

HOT PRAWN SOUP

Grate, or pound in a mortar, a de-seeded GREEN CHILLI and a small piece of peeled ROOT GINGER, and add a crushed clove of GARLIC. Mix with a tablespoonful of olive oil and heat in a covered pan. Add a stick of finely diced CELERY and cook until transparent. Stir in 3–4 oz/75–100g shelled North Atlantic PRAWNS, a tablespoonful of TAMARI* and a CARROT cut into julienne strips. Add enough FISH or VEGETABLE STOCK to cover and cook, covered, for 25 minutes. Add 2 oz/50g EGG NOODLES or vermicelli and simmer for a further 5–6 minutes.

---

* Tamari is similar to, but stronger tasting than, soy or shoyu sauce; it differs from them in having a longer fermentation period and a lower salt content, and in being free from wheat, so it is useful for coeliacs and others who have to avoid wheat.

PINEAPPLE AND PRAWN SALAD

Pineapples halved horizontally, hollowed out and filled with vegetable or fruit salads may be rather ostentatious, or old hat, but they do look attractive and exotic so don't be put off if you are 'spoiling yourself' at home or feel like spending some time fiddling around in the kitchen – actually it's quite speedy to do.

Using a sharp knife, remove the centre from half a PINE-APPLE and cube the flesh, discarding any woody central core but use it if it is soft. Mix with the pineapple some de-seeded BLACK GRAPES and about 4 oz/100g shelled North Atlantic PRAWNS. Toss in a dressing made from thick NATURAL YOGHURT seasoned with sea salt, freshly ground black pepper and a squeeze of LEMON or lime juice. Pile into the pineapple 'shell'.

SMOKED MACKEREL AND APPLE SALAD

Skin a SMOKED MACKEREL fillet and flake into large pieces. Dice half a red and half a green APPLE and a CELERY stick. For the dressing, mix together some NATURAL YOGHURT, MAYONNAISE, LEMON JUICE and seasoning. Toss the ingredients in the dressing, adding a handful of RAISINS. Serve with shredded LETTUCE and/or Granary BREAD.

Game and
Poultry

A game calendar

If you are interested in the game recipes, you will want to know when fresh game is in season; so here is a calendar to help you. Although the calendar is comprehensive there are not recipes in this book for every kind of game, but it is well worthwhile to experiment for yourself. There are many types of small game which make an ideal dish for one. It should also be genuinely free-range meat.

Grouse
12 AUGUST to 10 DECEMBER

Snipe
12 AUGUST to 31 JANUARY

Partridge
1 SEPTEMBER to 1 FEBRUARY

Wild Duck
1 SEPTEMBER to 31 JANUARY

Pheasant
1 OCTOBER to 1 FEBRUARY

Woodcock
31 OCTOBER to 1 FEBRUARY

Venison, hare, rabbit and pigeon are available all year round.

TYPICAL WEIGHTS

Poussin: from 14 oz/400g to 1½ lb/675g.

Quail: from 4 oz/100g to 6 oz/175g.

Guinea fowl: from 2 lb/850g to 2½ lb/1¼kg.

Hare saddles: from 1 lb/450g to 1¾ lb/800g.

QUAIL WITH POTATO AND TURNIP DAUPHINOISE

Thinly slice three medium-sized POTATOES and two small young TURNIPS. Heat a tablespoonful of olive oil in an ovenproof casserole or *petite marmite* and gently sauté two cloves of crushed GARLIC (do not brown). Add the potato and turnip slices. Season them, and stir in ¼ pint/150ml skimmed MILK and two rounded tablespoons of *CRÈME FRAÎCHE*. Cover with the lid and transfer to a moderate oven (350°F/180°C/Gas 4). Cook for 45 minutes. Remove the lid, increase the heat to 400°F/200°C/Gas 6 and place the prepared QUAIL on top of the vegetables. Cook for a further 30 minutes until the quail is golden brown. Serve with a green SALAD.

DUCK BREAST WITH APRICOTS

Halve six fresh APRICOTS and remove the stones, but do not skin. Grill lightly on each side, then arrange in the bottom of the grill pan beneath a DUCK BREAST where they will keep warm and be flavoured by the juices from the duck. If the duck breast has not been skinned there is no need to baste it while it grills for about 20 minutes. If it does require basting, use a mixture of olive oil and SHERRY VINEGAR. Sprinkle the duck and apricots with a little PAPRIKA before serving. Serve hot with RICE.

QUAIL ON TOAST

Roasting brings out the best flavour in QUAIL. It's usual to serve one quail per person, but you might like to roast a brace, or more, and keep the remainder for the next day. Being small, quail brown quickly; you can protect the breast with a slice of BACON, or cover with greaseproof paper for some of the cooking time. Either roast for 20–30 minutes in a hot oven, preheated to 425°F/220°C/Gas 7, or roast on a spit for 30–40 minutes. The quail is cooked if the juices run clear when it is pierced with a sharp knife.

When the quail is ready, toast slices of French BREAD and

spread with OLIVE PÂTÉ or pesto. Garnish with WATERCRESS and slices of ORANGE and serve the quail on the toast.

BONED STUFFED QUAIL

You can buy QUAIL that have been boned (except for the wings, of course) and then stuff them and steam them on a trivet or steaming-basket over stock for about 25 minutes. Or you can roast them as for Quail on Toast, above, or on a bed of vegetables as for Medallion of Venison, below. Each quail will take about 3 oz/75g of stuffing. Use either a traditional stuffing based on ground lean PORK (rather than sausagemeat) or ground nuts and fresh breadcrumbs mixed with chopped HERBS, ONION, and BREADCRUMBS or cooked rice, or use a ready-made chilled stuffing from a supermarket if you can find one to your taste.

MEDALLION OF VENISON

Medallions are brilliant for dinner for one. The small round cutlets of prime meat are trimmed of all fat and are just the right size for slimline eating – about 3 oz/75g each. If you have time, you could follow one of Anton Mosimann's suggestions for seasoning medallions. Crush some JUNIPER BERRIES (only about two or three for each medallion) and sprinkle them over the VENISON. Then cover the medallions and leave them in the fridge for a couple of hours. (I also like to use green or pink peppercorns for seasoning in the same way.)

Assemble a selection of vegetables such as COURGETTES, baby SWEETCORN, CARROTS, LEEKS, mange-tout PEAS, champignon MUSHROOMS and crinkly green CABBAGE, and cut them into julienne strips. Put the vegetables in a non-stick or heavy-based pan, adding a little VEGETABLE or MEAT STOCK, and simmer for 5 minutes. Arrange the medallions on top of the vegetables and cover. Cook until the meat is done to your liking – 5 or 6 minutes will leave it nicely pink inside.

POUSSIN WITH ORANGE STUFFING

POUSSINS are larger than quail and you will probably find they are just too big for one, yet too small for comfort and peace of mind if you have a guest to dinner. Persevere alone and use the remainder for a packed lunch . . .

To make the stuffing; heat a little olive oil in a heavy pan and brown a teaspoonful of WHITE MUSTARD SEEDS and a small pinch of CUMIN SEEDS – be careful, as they jump around! Chop a stick of CELERY and a medium-sized new POTATO and add to the seeds. Blanch the rind of half an organic ORANGE (I use organic citrus peel to avoid sprays, waxes and other nasties that are used on the skins, although one such additive, mineral hydrocarbon (mineral oil), has recently been banned). Add to the mixture, together with two skinned TOMATOES. Cover the pan and leave to cook for about 12 minutes, stirring to prevent sticking. Remove the pan from the heat, take out the rind from the stuffing and put it in the body cavity of the bird. Stir one tablespoonful of fresh wholemeal BREADCRUMBS, or cooked brown rice which gives a slightly nicer texture, into the stuffing. Stuff the poussin and put the bird on a tray in a roasting pan. Cover with greaseproof paper and roast in the oven preheated to 425°F/220°C/Gas 7 for 30 minutes, removing the paper for the last 15 minutes to brown the poussin. Serve with brown RICE and a GREEN VEGETABLE.

TANDOORI CHICKEN THIGHS

Blend in a food processor some TOMATO PURÉE, crushed cloves of GARLIC, grated ROOT GINGER, and quarter of a teaspoon of each of the following: GROUND CUMIN, CHILLI POWDER, GARAM MASALA, plus enough NATURAL YOGHURT and a little LEMON JUICE to make a thick paste. Cut the skin from the CHICKEN THIGHS and coat with the paste. Cover and leave in the fridge for at least 2 hours. Bake in a hot oven, 400°F/200°C/Gas 6, for about 30 minutes.

CHICKEN KEBABS

Take a skinned and boned CHICKEN BREAST and cut into bite-sized pieces. If you are planning ahead, marinate the chicken in a couple of tablespoons of olive oil mixed with one of LEMON JUICE and (this is optional) fresh HERBS of your choice. Slice a COURGETTE, a RED or GREEN PEPPER and a small ONION, cutting them also into bite-size pieces to fit on to kebab skewers. Either blanch them briefly, or put into a microwave dish with a lid and cook on Full power for 5 minutes, stirring once or twice. Thread the meat and vegetables on to the skewer and grill for 10 minutes, turning often – there is no need to baste with fat. Serve with warm PITTA BREAD (heat in the microwave), SALAD and/or brown RICE.

TURKEY ESCALOPES

Turkey escalopes are sold by some butchers and poulterers, or in supermarket packs – put any you don't use in the freezer. In a heavy-based pan cook a small diced ONION and four sliced MUSHROOMS in their own steam until soft (about 5 minutes). If you have a bottle of WHITE WINE open, add half a wineglassful; allow most to evaporate. Remove the pan from the heat and stir in four tablespoons of DOUBLE CREAM; return to a gentle heat and stir for a couple of minutes. Keep the sauce warm. Lightly cook about four TURKEY ESCALOPES in a little unsalted BUTTER, or brush them with LEMON JUICE and olive oil and put them under the grill for 3–4 minutes. Arrange on a serving dish and spoon the sauce over them. Serve with plain RICE or noodles.

HONEY AND LIME CHICKEN THIGHS

This delicious idea is a variation on one invented for *Taste*, by Shirley Gill. Skin two or three CHICKEN THIGHS (this removes the layer of fat which lies just below the skin) and put them on a rack in the grill pan. Put two tablespoons of CLEAR HONEY in a saucepan or microwave jug and add the juice of a LIME; heat briefly so that the two are blended. Brush the mixture over the chicken as it cooks under the grill. Serve with RICE or a green SALAD (you can also use lime juice in the vinaigrette dressing).

DEVILLED POUSSIN

For this dish you need to make a simple marinade and steep the poussin in it for at least 2 hours. To make the marinade: place a couple of skinned (not really vital but it makes a smoother sauce) ripe TOMATOES in the food processor with a tablespoonful each of WORCESTERSHIRE SAUCE, SHERRY VINEGAR and LEMON JUICE, plus a dessertspoonful of MUSCOVADO or demerara SUGAR and a pinch of CAYENNE or pimento red pepper. Blend well.

Now halve the POUSSIN by placing on your meat chopping board, breast side down, and cutting along the backbone with poultry shears or kitchen scissors. Turn over and continue to cut in half. If you want to be 'extra healthy', cut the skin off the bird. Place the poussin halves in a baking dish and spoon the marinade over them. Cover the dish and refrigerate for at least 2 hours or until needed. Then bake for 30–35 minutes in a hot oven (400°F/200°C/Gas 6). Serve with RICE or potatoes, and/or SALAD.

PIGEON WITH CINNAMON RICE

This is an ideal 'one-pot' meal. The pigeon is cooked on a bed of rice, and all the juices remain in the pan to give it a succulent flavour. First wash 2 oz/50g brown RICE. Brown the cleaned PIGEON in a little olive oil in a heavy saucepan. Remove, and sauté a medium-sized diced ONION and a SWEET PEPPER in the pan. Stir in the rice, plus a small handful of lightly toasted split or flaked ALMONDS, a tablespoonful of CURRANTS and a pinch of GROUND CINNAMON. Put the pigeon on top of the rice and add enough STOCK to cover the rice and go a little way up the pigeon – don't drown the bird! Cover with a well-fitting lid and let the dish cook gently in its own steam for about 40 minutes. Check from time to time to make sure it hasn't boiled dry. Serve with steamed CABBAGE flavoured with freshly grated NUTMEG.

Meat

*Before tucking in to the recipes in this
section please refer to the notes on organic
meat on page 20.*

KIDNEYS IN SHERRY

As quick and simple to cook as Leopold Bloom's celebrated kidneys, but with a certain additional finesse. Somehow kidneys are a dish to be eaten either on one's own or in a tremendously posh restaurant. Skin two LAMB'S KIDNEYS, halve, and remove the white core using kitchen scissors. Gently sauté in a little unsalted BUTTER until just firm, then remove from the pan and keep warm. Add two sliced SHALLOTS to the pan and cook until soft. Stir in a little white FLOUR and add a small amount of VEGETABLE STOCK – about two-thirds of a wineglassful. Stir constantly, over a low flame, until the sauce thickens, add a tablespoonful of SHERRY and return the kidneys to the pan. Heat through, season, and serve with brown RICE or creamed potato.

GAMMON WITH GRAPES

Brush a succulent GAMMON STEAK with CLEAR HONEY and begin to grill it slowly. Meanwhile melt together in a saucepan a couple of tablespoons of dark MUSCOVADO SUGAR and a little more than that of GRAPE JUICE. Add half a wineglass of CIDER and a generous pinch of GROUND ALLSPICE. Simmer for about 5 minutes, then stir in ½ oz/25g unsalted BUTTER. In another pan, lightly sauté about thirty GRAPES in ½ oz/25g unsalted butter. Keep the sauce and the grapes warm while you finish grilling the gammon, turning it once and brushing the second side of it with honey. Transfer the grilled gammon to a serving dish, put the grapes beside it, and pour over the sauce. Serve with boiled or steamed RICE.

BEEFBURGERS

Home-made burgers are very simple to make and have a much better flavour than bought ones. You can either buy lean STEAK and mince it yourself at home, or buy extra lean MINCE. The classic burger is just seasoned ground meat grilled or char-grilled over a flame, but you can make some interesting additions to home-made burgers. To about 8 oz/225g meat add the following ingredients, or as many of them as you can muster: grated ONION, ready-made MUSTARD, grated CARROT, chopped TOMATO, tomato or mushroom KETCHUP or purée, fresh HERBS, sea salt and freshly ground black pepper. Fry the burgers in the usual way.

You can also use ground or minced LAMB or CHICKEN for a more unusual variant, with Indian CURRY SPICES or Mediterranean herbs.

ONE-POT LIVER

Liver, like other offal, is good as a meal for one. In a group of people there is often one who does not like it, but to its devotees it makes a delicious and nourishing dish. It cooks very quickly, too. Slice one or two scrubbed, unpeeled POTATOES and a peeled ONION (more than one, if they are small) and arrange in layers in a lightly oiled, heavy-based pan. Lay the sliced LIVER on top – about 6 oz/175g will be enough – and season with sea salt and freshly ground black pepper. Add a layer of sliced COOKING APPLE and sprinkle with a very little chopped fresh SAGE. Top with a layer of sliced potato. In a heavy pan with a well-fitting lid, this should cook in its own steam in about 25 minutes, but add a little stock if you are nervous about it.

LAMB KEBABS

You can make lamb kebabs in the same way as Chicken Kebabs (page 56). Instead of marinating in olive oil and lemon juice, try NATURAL YOGHURT mixed with ground FRESH CHILLIES and GARLIC, or red wine and garlic. Follow the method for Chicken Kebabs – again, there is no need to baste with fat.

GROUND MEAT KEBABS

Mostly we think of using bite-size pieces of lamb fillet for kebabs, but seasoned ground (minced) lamb, beef or pork are equally delicious. You can mould the meat into small balls to thread on to the skewer, or shape a larger piece, as they do in

Turkey, which can be almost the length of the skewer itself. Mix 4–6 oz/100–175g GROUND MEAT with some finely grated ONION, a little olive oil and LEMON JUICE and some fresh THYME. There are many other variations and additions; you could use ground cinnamon, cloves and allspice for a Middle Eastern flavour, or Indian-style spices such as ground cumin, coriander or garam masala. Some bulgur or cracked wheat, pre-soaked in water for 10 minutes, will extend the meat and add fibre (or make the basis for vegetarian kebabs). If necessary, add a beaten free-range EGG to bind the mixture. Form around the skewers and grill or barbecue for 5–6 minutes, turning frequently to brown the kebabs evenly. Serve on a bed of cooked or canned TOMATOES.

LAMARGE (TURKISH PIZZA)

This is a mince topping on a very thin, pizza-type base which is more like an Arabic or pitta bread than an Italian pizza dough. However, you can use a ready-made pizza base and top it with a mixture of GROUND (MINCED) LAMB or beef combined with finely grated ONION, chopped CHILLIES, sliced TOMATOES, seasoning and finely chopped PARSLEY. This kind of pizza is often folded in half, or loosely rolled up, and brushed with melted BUTTER or oil before being baked in a moderate to hot oven (around 375°F/190°C/Gas 5) for 20–25 minutes.

CHINESE CHOPS

Choose a couple of lean rib LAMB CHOPS and trim off the fat. Marinate for at least half-an-hour, preferably for an hour, in two tablespoons of HOI SIN or naturally brewed soy sauce, mixed with a tablespoonful of ORANGE JUICE. Grill under a hot grill until golden but not overcooked. Serve with minted salad POTATOES such as pink fir apple.

BEEF TOURNEDOS

Instead of buying a piece of forerib or silverside to roast, ask your butcher to cut you a TOURNEDOS OF BEEF FILLET, or look out for them in supermarkets where they may be sold in packs of two or four – unused ones can be frozen. This is an expensive cut of beef, but tender and delicious with no waste. Tournedos are usually dressed with a little beef fat which can easily be removed.

Either grill the seasoned tournedos without added fat, or lightly fry it in unsalted BUTTER or olive oil for two minutes on each side. For a more ambitious version, wrap it in PUFF PASTRY for a miniature *bœuf en croûte*. Lay the tournedos on one half of a sheet of pastry with a sliced MUSHROOM above and below the meat, fold the pastry over and pinch the edges together so that the tournedos is quite enclosed. (Alternatively, spread the base and top of the beef with pâté before wrapping in the *croûte*.) Glaze the pastry with a little beaten free-range EGG and bake for 10 minutes at a high temperature (425°F/220°C/Gas 7).

STIR-FRY BEEF

You need only a small amount of BEEF FILLET (about 4 oz/100g), or a thinly sliced steak, for adding to a stir-fry – the main interest is in the wonderfully colourful vegetables and the delicate flavour of the dish. Cut the beef into fine strips and, if you have time, marinate it (ideally for up to 4 hours, but 30 minutes is better than nothing) in some BLACK BEAN or OYSTER SAUCE, or make your own marinade with a couple of tablespoons each of ORANGE JUICE and naturally brewed SOY (or shoyu) SAUCE, plus some freshly grated ROOT GINGER and a clove of GARLIC. Prepare a selection of vegetables by cutting them into fine strips: for example, a RED, GREEN or YELLOW PEPPER, a large CARROT, and CABBAGE or CHINESE LEAVES. BABY SWEETCORN and MANGE-TOUT are perfect as they are. Now heat a small amount of VEGETABLE OIL in a wok or large saucepan and stir-fry the meat for just a few seconds until brown. Add the rest of the ingredients (the carrots first, and the rest in order of 'hardness') and stir-fry for 2 or 3 minutes. If you decide to use BEAN-SPROUTS, cook these at the end for no more than a minute, just to heat through. The vegetables should be crisp. If you like, you can pour over the marinade sauce when the vegetables are cooked. This makes an excellent meal on its own, but serve with steamed brown RICE if you would like an accompaniment.

Chicken liver pilau

A lovely combination of nutty brown rice and chicken livers, cooked with pine kernels and currants. Like most Middle Eastern food, it is best served slightly warm. Wash 2 oz/50g brown RICE and pressure-cook for 6 minutes or boil for 20 minutes. Drain well. Heat a tablespoonful of olive oil and sauté a tablespoonful of PINE KERNELS. Add the cooked rice, a tablespoonful of CURRANTS and 4 oz/100g chopped CHICKEN LIVERS and cook for a further 5 minutes, stirring well. Season to taste, and serve.

Pasta

Pasta increases three times in volume during cooking, so start with a large pan of boiling water. For a single portion you need 2–3 oz/50–75g dry weight of pasta, depending on your appetite. Fresh pasta is not dehydrated and will not increase in volume in the same way; you will therefore need to cook more – about 6 oz/175g for a single portion. Fresh pasta cooks in 2–3 minutes (unused keeps only 2 days).

This quantity of either dried or fresh pasta is cooked in about 1 pint/600ml fast-boiling water. Slowly stir the pasta as you add it to the water (this is particularly necessary in the case of dry pasta) to prevent it sticking together – a teaspoonful of vegetable oil added to the water helps to prevent sticking – and start timing the cooking when it comes back to the boil. Cooking time depends on the type and brand of pasta, so read the instructions on the pack. Check before the cooking time is complete so that you don't overcook. Pasta should be eaten *al dente* – tender but still firm. Strain and serve immediately, or use in one of the recipes below.

RIGATONI WITH BACON

Cook about 3 oz/75g RIGATONI (or similar quill-shaped pasta) in plenty of slightly salted boiling water until just *al dente*. Grill 2 rashers of smoked back BACON until crisp. Meanwhile gently warm 2 oz/50g grated PARMESAN CHEESE in a saucepan, stirring occasionally. Drain the pasta and pour the cheese over it. Season with freshly ground black pepper and add 1 tablespoon chopped continental PARSLEY. Mix together lightly and serve at once.

SPAGHETTI VONGOLE

Cook about 3 oz/75g wholemeal SPAGHETTI in plenty of slightly salted boiling water until just *al dente*. While the spaghetti is boiling, sauté (but do not brown) a crushed clove of GARLIC and two diced SHALLOTS in a tablespoonful of olive oil. Add 2–3 oz/50–75g defrosted frozen CLAMS and cook gently for 3 minutes, stirring constantly. Add half a wineglass of dry white

WINE and continue cooking over a high heat for a further 3 minutes. Drain the spaghetti and transfer to a serving dish, top with the clams and serve at once.

RICOTTA TORTELLONI WITH TOMATO SAUCE

Cook about 5 oz/150g ready-prepared TORTELLONI stuffed with RICOTTA CHEESE as instructed on the pack. While the pasta is cooking, in a saucepan sauté a couple of SHALLOTS or a small diced onion, and a stick of CELERY. Liquidize, or pass through a sieve, two peeled TOMATOES and add them to the shallots and celery. Continue cooking for a couple of minutes. Then add the drained tortelloni to the tomato sauce. Serve with freshly grated PARMESAN CHEESE.

SPAGHETTI WITH PESTO SPINACH AND PINE NUTS

For this recipe you can also use finer pastas such as tagliolini, or even the 'soup pasta', vermicelli. Wash about 4 oz/100g fresh SPINACH and trim off any thick stalks. As the spinach will retain some moisture after washing, there is no need to add more water. Cook it until it is just tender, drain well, and keep it warm. Boil 2–3 oz/50–75g PASTA as instructed on the pack. When cooked, drain and toss with the spinach and a large tablespoonful of PESTO sauce. Put in a serving dish and scatter a small quantity of PINE KERNELS and some chopped fresh BASIL on top. Serve with freshly grated PARMESAN CHEESE.

MEATBALLS WITH TAGLIATELLE

Put 4 oz/100g GROUND (MINCED) LAMB or pork in the food processor and blend with a pinch of CINNAMON, just a hint of GROUND CLOVES, sea salt and freshly ground black pepper. Mould the blended mixture into small balls and lightly brown them in a pan with a little olive oil. Add two ripe, roughly chopped TOMATOES and some freshly chopped continental PARSLEY. Cover the pan to allow the meatballs to finish cooking in their own steam for about 6 minutes, then keep them warm. Cook the TAGLIA-TELLE as instructed on the pack, drain, and arrange in a serving dish. Top with the meatballs in their sauce. Serve with a green salad.

RAVIOLI WITH BROCCOLI

Boil 4 oz/100g RAVIOLI (filled with either meat or cheese) according to instructions on the pack. Meanwhile, make a sauce. Crush a clove of GARLIC and sauté in a little olive oil. Add two chopped TOMATOES broken up well with the back of a wooden spoon, and a couple of ANCHOVY FILLETS, also crushed, or a teaspoonful of anchovy purée. Cook for a few minutes, and then keep the sauce warm. Steam or boil 4 oz/100g BROCCOLI cut into small florets. Mix the cooked and drained ravioli with the sauce and serve with the broccoli.

PEPPER AND MUSHROOM CARBONARA

Boil about 2 oz/50g wholemeal PASTA SHELLS in plenty of water until *al dente*, then drain. Finely shred half a RED PEPPER, thinly slice a small ONION, crush a clove of GARLIC and quarter a few MUSHROOMS. Sauté these gently in olive oil until they soften, then increase the heat and add the pasta. Quickly whisk 1 free-range EGG with a tablespoonful of CREAM, and season with sea salt and freshly ground black pepper. Remove the vegetables from the heat and stir in the egg mixture. Keep stirring over a low heat as the egg scrambles. Mix in some freshly chopped continental PARSLEY and serve at once.

SMOKED SALMON WITH DILL

Boil 2–3 oz/50–75g wholemeal PASTA SHELLS until *al dente*. In a saucepan, gently warm about ¼ pint/150ml *FROMAGE FRAIS* (do not boil) and stir into it 2–3 oz/50–75g SMOKED SALMON, cut into shreds. Add some LEMON JUICE and freshly ground black pepper, plus some finely chopped DILL. Drain the pasta, toss immediately into the sauce and serve.

PASTA PROVENÇALE

Slice a small ONION into rings and cook with a crushed clove of GARLIC and half a diced GREEN PEPPER (remove the stem and seeds) in a covered saucepan in their own steam for about 5 minutes. Drain a small can of ANCHOVIES, pat off excess oil with kitchen paper and add about half of them to the pan with two teaspoons of CAPERS and two roughly chopped TOMATOES. Leave to simmer for about 10 minutes while you cook some PASTA of your choice, for example shells, twists or penne, in a separate pan. Drain the pasta. Stir a tablespoonful of freshly chopped BASIL into the sauce and spoon it over the pasta.

Salads and
Salad Meals

Mainly green salads

WILD SALAD

When I ordered my first Wild Salad in Boston, USA, I was quite disappointed at the tame thing that appeared; so here is a screamingly wild salad. Toss together a huge pile of ROCKET, PURSLANE, LAMB'S LETTUCE (corn salad), RED OAK-LEAF LETTUCE (*feuille de chêne*) and crispy PAIN DE SUCRE (sugar loaf – an elongated head of bright yellow leaves), or as many of them as you can find. (Supermarkets often sell a good selection in packs.) That really is a wild collection of saladings. Scatter with toasted chopped HAZELNUTS and serve with Hazelnut Dressing (page 86).

WILTED SALAD

If you are not feeling in a wild mood, then pour a warm salad dressing over the above and turn it into another American extravaganza . . . the wilted salad. Or use another not-quite-so-wild salad base: watercress or land cress, dandelion, spinach and assorted lettuce leaves.

AVOCADO SALAD WITH BEETROOT

These two vegetables make a deliciously rich contrast in colour and flavour, together with cooked green beans and an ounce or two of lightly roasted hazelnuts. First wash, top and tail some GREEN BEANS (2 oz/50g will be enough) and cook them until they are just tender. Leave them to cool. Then stone and peel half an AVOCADO (to slip off the peel, use a teaspoon to ease the skin away from the edges), slice and dress it at once in some LEMON JUICE to prevent browning. Dice some BEETROOT or use halved baby beetroot. Arrange the avocado, beetroot and beans in a shell of RADICCHIO and ROCKET leaves and scatter with the roasted HAZELNUTS. Dress with a Hazelnut Dressing (page 86).

Other colourful salads

GRILLED PEPPER AND AUBERGINE SALAD

Grill a RED and a GREEN (or yellow) PEPPER under a fierce heat so that the skins become slightly charred. Remove from the heat and slip off the blackened skins. Remove seeds and stalks and slice into chunks, not strips. At the same time, grill slices of AUBERGINE brushed with olive oil and seasoned with sea salt and freshly ground black pepper. Turn the aubergine slices to ensure even cooking and browning. Mix the peppers and the aubergine slices. The warm salad can be dressed in a vinaigrette, but it tastes good just as it is.

SEVEN-COLOUR NO-BORE SALAD

Another riotous American salad that uses the seven colour varieties of pepper available Stateside: chocolate, yellow, orange, purple, black and the standard red and green. Come to think of it, in Britain we also get Dutch orange peppers, so go one better . . .

The peppers are nicest grilled until the skin bubbles and blackens a little. Remove the skin, slice the peppers and serve with a vinaigrette dressing alongside grilled fish – perhaps a red or grey mullet.

TOMATO AND BASIL SALAD

This is a wonderful combination. Add to it the elements of a Greek salad, so that you have slices of ripe BEEFSTEAK TOMATO in a VINAIGRETTE (made with plenty of olive oil), choc-à-bloc with chopped BASIL leaves, topped with small cubes of FETA or Mozzarella CHEESE, and scattered with BLACK OLIVES. Garnish with whole basil leaves.

FRUITY SALAD

Although we think mainly in terms of vegetables for salads, fruit makes a summery addition at any time of the year. On a bed of shredded LETTUCE arrange segments of ORANGE and slices of BANANA, GREEN PEPPER, CELERY and CUCUMBER mixed with toasted flaked ALMONDS and tossed in a little MAYONNAISE, or Greek yoghurt seasoned with sea salt, freshly ground black pepper and lemon juice.

Fish salads

PRAWN SALAD

Cut julienne strips of raw CARROT and RED and YELLOW PEPPERS. Mix the vegetables with 4 oz/100g large North Atlantic PRAWNS. Arrange a bed of LETTUCE and RADICCHIO on your serving dish, top with a mound of prawns and vegetables and spoon over them a little Lemon Dressing (below).

LEMON DRESSING

Stir a teaspoonful of LEMON JUICE into half a small pot of NATURAL YOGHURT. Add sea salt, freshly ground black pepper and a teaspoonful of made ENGLISH MUSTARD. Stir in some freshly chopped PARSLEY.

CRAB AND GRAPEFRUIT SALAD

Not an original idea, but one that is well worth trying if it happens to be new to you. If you can dress a CRAB yourself, then go ahead; otherwise buy a ready-dressed one. Keep the brown meat for making sandwich fillings or using in a quiche or flan, and flake the white meat. Peel five or six GRAPEFRUIT segments (using a mixture of pink and standard grapefruit if you can) and arrange them with the crab meat on crunchy LETTUCE or batavia (escarole). Season lightly with a little PAPRIKA and offer yourself MAYONNAISE and crusty BREAD, separately.

TUNA AND BUTTER BEAN SALAD

Drain a small can of BUTTER BEANS and a small can of TUNA FISH in brine (both about 7 oz/200g, although you don't have to use all the contents at once). Finely slice half an ONION and quarter a ripe TOMATO. Place the beans on a serving dish and top with the flaked tuna and onion rings, arrange the tomato quarters round the edge, then scatter with freshly chopped PARSLEY. Serve with a VINAIGRETTE to which you have added some WHOLE-GRAIN MUSTARD.

WALNUT AND SALMON SALAD

Make an exciting salad combining leaves of FRISÉE, RED OAK-LEAF LETTUCE (*feuille de chêne*), BATAVIA (escarole), LAMB'S LETTUCE, CHICORY and BASIL, and mix into it wholemeal Croutons (page 87), WALNUT PIECES and slivers of SMOKED SALMON. Toss in a WALNUT DRESSING (page 86) the moment before you are ready to eat.

TUNA AND POTATO SALAD

The quality of the POTATOES is the key to success here. They should be waxy, not floury. Cook as many as you need (scrub or scrape – no need to peel), and let them cool. Dice them roughly and add 3–4 oz/75–100g drained and flaked TUNA in brine and a chopped free-range hard-boiled EGG. Scatter with chopped SPRING ONIONS and surround with slices of ripe TOMATO. Serve with a bowl of aïoli (page 98) or a simple mayonnaise.

SALADE NIÇOISE

– the famous salad 'in the style of Nice'. Start with a bed of shredded crisp LETTUCE and top with half a sliced GREEN PEPPER,

a couple of sliced ripe TOMATOES, a few whole small NEW PO-
TATOES, cooked and cooled (or slightly waxy maincrop varieties,
such as Cara, Carlingford, Charlotte, Desirée or Romano), thin
slices of ONION (optional), some BLACK OLIVES and large juicy
CAPERS. Drain a can of ANCHOVY FILLETS and pat off excess oil
with kitchen paper. Separate the fillets and add half of them to the
salad. Chop some fresh BASIL leaves and quarter a hard-boiled
free-range EGG, and garnish the salad with them. Dress with a
VINAIGRETTE using a higher proportion of olive oil than usual. A
crushed GARLIC clove can be added to the dressing.

FAGIOLI CON TONNO

A bean and tuna salad. Toss about 6–7 oz/175–200g cold
cooked WHITE BEANS such as borlotti (which you can buy in cans –
drain and rinse) with a little diced FENNEL and CELERY. Put the
mixture in the bottom of an attractive salad bowl. Top with a
small can of TUNA (in brine for weight-watchers – drain well and
flake with a fork), and a few BLACK OLIVES (a variety marinated in
garlic, herbs and spices add piquancy). Garnish with thin wedges
of TOMATO and slices of crispy RED-SKINNED ONION.

SWEDISH SILD (HERRING) SALAD

Make a basic green salad of LETTUCE and BATAVIA
(escarole). Then add a layer of sliced RADISH, diced BEETROOT and
diced cold cooked POTATO. Top with one or two ROLLMOP
HERRINGS or the contents of a small can of sild (herring marinated
in a variety of sauces, including mustard, soured cream or dill).
Garnish with a quartered hard-boiled free-range EGG and pickled
GHERKINS. Serve with rye crispbread.

MINTY PRAWN SALAD

Shred a bed of crunchy LETTUCE into an individual salad
bowl. Mix three tablespoons of GREEK YOGHURT with two teaspoons of LEMON JUICE, salt and freshly ground black pepper and

a tablespoonful of freshly chopped MINT. Pile 4 oz/100g large North Atlantic PRAWNS on the lettuce and top with the dressing. Serve with brown BREAD and BUTTER.

AVOCADO AND SALMON SALAD

Peel and stone half an AVOCADO and dress with LEMON JUICE to prevent browning. Slice thickly but keep the avocado in its original shape. Fill a piping bag with half a tub of SMOKED SALMON PÂTÉ and pipe the pâté between the slices of avocado. Serve with a large green SALAD and dressing of your choice.

COLD SALMON AND PEACH SALAD

Lightly poach a SALMON STEAK in a *COURT-BOUILLON* or fish stock and leave in the stock until completely cold. Lift the salmon carefully on to a serving dish and garnish with thin slices of half a ripe PEACH. Serve with a green SALAD of frisée, crisp BEAN-SPROUTS, sliced RADISH and the rest of the peach, diced, with a Sweet and Sour Dressing (below).

SWEET AND SOUR DRESSING

Put half a tablespoonful of naturally brewed SOY SAUCE, the juice of half an ORANGE and one tablespoonful of soy, corn or sunflower OIL in a clean screw-top jar and shake well. The dressing is a useful one to keep in the fridge. The little pots in which breakfast-size portions of preserves are sold are ideal for storing small quantities.

LANGOUSTINE AND GRAPEFRUIT SALAD

Poach four LANGOUSTINES in boiling water for 7 minutes, pour off the liquor and refresh under cold water. Make a salad of FRISÉE and RED OAK-LEAF LETTUCE (*feuille de chêne*) and toss in Hazelnut Dressing (page 86). Prepare segments from about one-third of a PINK GRAPEFRUIT. Shell three of the langoustines and arrange the grapefruit and shellfish on top of the salad, leaving the fourth langoustine, still in its shell, to garnish the dish. Serve with brown BREAD and BUTTER.

COURGETTES AND PRAWN MAYONNAISE

Wash two large COURGETTES and steam or boil for 6 minutes. Remove, and plunge into cold water to refresh. While they are cooling, make the mayonnaise by pouring into a liquidizer, or beating by hand, 8 fl. oz/250ml olive or sunflower oil, a free-range EGG yolk, and a dessertspoonful of made MUSTARD (whole-grain if you don't mind the speckled appearance, French if you like it mild and English if you like it hot). Add some freshly chopped DILL and season to taste. Cut the courgettes along their length, scooping out most of the flesh but leaving enough to form a shell. Mix 2–3 oz/50–75g shelled North Atlantic PRAWNS with a quarter of the mayonnaise and pile into the shells. (The remainder of the mayonnaise can be kept in the fridge.) Garnish with feathery sprigs of dill. Store unused mayonnaise – also delicious with WALNUT OIL – in the fridge, covered.

Meat salads

ROAST CHICKEN AND GOAT'S CHEESE

Slice 4 oz/100g cold roast CHICKEN or smoked chicken. Serve with a small quantity of crumbled GOAT'S CHEESE on a bed of mixed salad containing crunchy LETTUCE, CHERRY TOMATOES, sliced RED PEPPER (with the skin charred under the grill and removed), and some darker green leaves such as LAMB'S LETTUCE or watercress. Dress with a VINAIGRETTE to which you have added freshly chopped OREGANO or marjoram. Eat with crusty French BREAD.

SMOKED GOOSE BREAST SALAD

Make a salad of FRISÉE and RED OAK-LEAF LETTUCE (*feuille de chêne*), 2–3 sliced SPRING ONIONS and 3–4 oz/75–100g cold cooked BROAD BEANS. Toss in a VINAIGRETTE made with plenty of olive oil, stirring in one tablespoonful of freshly chopped PARSLEY at the same time. Top with finely sliced SMOKED GOOSE BREAST (about 2 oz/50g). Garnish with thin slices of truffle (optional).

Miscellaneous salads

GREEK POTATO SALAD

This can only be described as a delicious garlic-potato paste. It's not worth making a very small amount, so either have it when friends are coming or keep the remainder in the fridge for use over the next few days. The authentic way to cook the dish, as described by Greek cookery writer Alkmini Chaitow who first introduced me to this dish, is first to boil about 1 lb/450g POTATOES with their skins on; when they are cool enough to handle, slip off the skins and mash the potatoes with four cloves of crushed GARLIC, four tablespoons of olive oil, some sea salt and the juice of a LEMON. Pass the potato through a food processor for the smoothest results. Garnish with freshly chopped PARSLEY and BLACK OLIVES.

MUSHROOM SOY SALAD

Wild mushrooms may be all the rage (or they were when I was eating my way around this book!) but three other equally delicious varieties are available in the shops for those mere mortals without access to restaurant suppliers. All you need is 2 oz/50g each of brown CHAMPIGNON, SHI'TAKE and OYSTER MUSHROOMS. Sauté a little crushed GARLIC in SESAME OIL and add to the pan a tablespoonful each of OYSTER SAUCE, naturally brewed SOY SAUCE and DRY SHERRY, and the juice of half an

ORANGE. The whole mushrooms should then be added and cooked for 2–3 minutes: stir all the time they are cooking. Garnish with sliced SPRING ONIONS and serve just warm.

TABOULLEH

Soak some BULGUR or cracked wheat in water for about 10 minutes or according to the instructions on the packet. While it is soaking, prepare the salad vegetables: dice a RED-SKINNED ONION and some CUCUMBER; chop some PARSLEY and MINT leaves. Mix the vegetables and herbs with the grain and toss in VINAIGRETTE with a crushed clove of GARLIC (optional). Serve at room temperature, or chill.

PEAR AND BLUE CHEESE SALAD

Wash and dry an attractive selection of salad greens such as those listed for Wild Salad (page 72) or Walnut and Salmon Salad (page 75), plus some RADICCHIO leaves. Add 2 oz/50g diced BLEU D'AUVERGNE CHEESE and a peeled, cored and diced PEAR such as Comice (ripe but still firm), briefly tossed in LEMON JUICE.

PATLIKAN (TURKISH AUBERGINE SALAD)

We might call this a dip or even a vegetable pâté, but in Turkey it is called a salad and scooped up with warm-from-the-oven pitta-style bread. The AUBERGINE is first cooked and is then made into a paste. The best way to do this is to put the aubergine under the grill, which will char the skin and give it a nice smoky flavour – as near as you will get to a Turkish aubergine cooked over an open fire or barbecue. Or you can cook it in the microwave on Full power for about 4 minutes, turning once or twice, or in the oven. If you are using the grill, this will take about 12 minutes; turn the aubergine frequently. When it is cool enough to handle, scoop the flesh from the skin, put it in the liquidizer with a tablespoonful of olive oil, two teaspoons of LEMON JUICE and a crushed clove of GARLIC. Blend for a few moments, transfer to a serving bowl and garnish with chopped PARSLEY and BLACK OLIVES.

TURKISH BROWN BEAN SALAD

Like the Turkish Aubergine Salad, this is similar to a vegetable pâté. Wash and soak about 4 oz/100g FAVA BEANS, or any other dried brown beans. Cook them in plenty of boiling water until tender – this will take about 1½ hours – or pressure-cook for about 25 minutes. Drain the cooked beans and transfer to the liquidizer with the juice of half a LEMON, a tablespoonful of olive oil, a small pot of NATURAL YOGHURT and seasoning of sea salt, freshly ground black pepper and, if you wish, a spice such as GROUND CUMIN or another of your choice. Serve with PITTA BREAD and *crudités* such as RADISHES and CUCUMBER.

SALSIFY, CAULIFLOWER AND STILTON SALAD

Scrub two SALSIFY roots, peel, then boil or steam until tender (about 25 minutes) and allow to cool. Cut into strips and place on a bed of crunchy green leaves such as BATAVIA (escarole) and white or red CHICORY. Scatter with some tiny florets of raw CAULIFLOWER. Lastly, sprinkle with a little crumbly blue STILTON CHEESE.

FETA SALAD

If you love the tangy, slightly salty flavour of FETA CHEESE, crumble 2–3 oz/50–75g of it on top of a dish of shredded crispy LETTUCE which has in turn been topped with a large, juicy, thinly sliced BEEFSTEAK TOMATO and half a cold, cooked and cubed AUBERGINE, both generously doused in a VINAIGRETTE made with plenty of olive oil. Sprinkle with black pepper and scatter with a few plump and juicy BLACK OLIVES. (Cook the aubergine under the grill – see Turkish Aubergine Salad, page 80 – or, for speed, pierce the skin and microwave on Full power for 5–6 minutes. Remove and cube carefully because it will be very hot.)

MOZZARELLA AND TOMATO
WITH BASIL

Slice two ripe TOMATOES. Peel and slice half an AVOCADO, then sprinkle with LEMON JUICE to prevent it discolouring. Slice about 2 oz/50g MOZZARELLA CHEESE. Arrange the three ingredients on a serving dish. Make a VINAIGRETTE, adding a few freshly chopped BASIL leaves and saving one or two whole leaves for a garnish. Pour the dressing over the salad and serve with warm, crusty Italian BREAD.

ITALIAN MELON SALAD

Using a Parisienne cutter, scoop some marble-sized balls from a ripe, fragrant MELON. Make a green salad of COS LETTUCE and BATAVIA (escarole) and toss in a VINAIGRETTE made with a generous proportion of olive oil. Stir in 2 or 3 sliced ARTICHOKE HEARTS (these can be bought canned, or from a delicatessen). Arrange some thin strips of PARMA HAM, the melon balls and half a sliced PEACH on top of the salad.

Salades Tièdes
(or Warm Salads)

CHICKEN LIVER SALAD

Take a selection of SALAD LEAVES (such as red oak-leaf (*feuille de chêne*), radicchio, lamb's lettuce, frisée, etc., which can be bought in packs in many supermarkets); rinse and dry the salad, and dress it with Hazelnut Dressing (page 86). Slice 4–6 oz/100–175g CHICKEN LIVERS and sauté gently in unsalted BUTTER for a couple of minutes until cooked, but still pink inside. (If you have stopped cooking chicken products lightly since reports of an increased incidence of salmonella, then wait until you are again confident before trying the recipe rather than spoil the dish by overcooking the liver.) Place on absorbent kitchen paper to remove excess fat and arrange on top of the salad leaves. Sprinkle with a tablespoonful of lightly toasted whole HAZELNUTS.

CONTINENTAL LENTIL SALAD

Boil 2 oz/50g continental WHOLE GREEN LENTILS in twice their volume of water until tender and cooked but not mushy (about 15 minutes). Drain, if the water has not all been absorbed. Toss at once in a VINAIGRETTE made with a generous proportion of olive oil, which has had two cloves of crushed GARLIC added. Serve the warm lentils in an attractive bowl on a bed of crisp LETTUCE, garnished with whole small NEW POTATOES (hot or cold), a quartered hard-boiled free-range EGG and CHERRY TOMATOES.

OYSTER MUSHROOM AND GREEN BEAN SALAD

Poach two or three (depending on size) OYSTER MUSH-ROOMS in a little water to which you have added a teaspoonful of naturally brewed SOY SAUCE or anchovy essence. Allow to cool a little, remove and pat dry on absorbent kitchen paper. Halve and remove the pips from about 10 GREEN GRAPES. Boil or steam 3 oz/75g FRENCH BEANS until *al dente*, rinse quickly under cold water to stop cooking, but not to make the beans completely cold. Drain thoroughly. Cut the beans into bite-size pieces. Toss the grapes, beans and a basic green salad of LETTUCE and RED OAK-LEAF in a Hazelnut Dressing (page 86) and arrange on the serving dish. Top with the mushrooms.

PUY LENTILS WITH SMOKED DUCK

PUY LENTILS are small, greyish-brown whole lentils from the Haute-Loire region of France. Prepare 2 oz/50g of them as for Continental Lentil Salad (page 84). While they are still warm, toss in a VINAIGRETTE made with a good proportion of olive oil, and just a little garlic (optional, this time!). Place in a salad bowl and top with thin slices of SMOKED DUCK BREAST. Smoked goose (*oie* in French) is just as delicious.

WALNUT AND CAMEMBERT SALAD

Make a mixed green salad of LETTUCE, ROCKET* and PURS-LANE* (buy LAMB'S LETTUCE if the last two are unavailable), LOLLO ROSSO (or other interesting frilly red/green lettuce variety), and 2 oz/50g chopped WALNUT HALVES or PIECES. Cut one or two slices of WALNUT BREAD (the recipe in the Roux Brothers' *New Classic Cuisine*, Macdonald, 1983, new edn 1989, is the best I have used) and warm them in the microwave on Medium for 20 seconds. Warm an unwrapped individual portion of CAMEMBERT CHEESE (1½–2 oz/40–50g) in the microwave on Medium for 30 seconds. Toss the salad in Walnut Dressing (below) and serve with the warm bread and cheese.

---

* Both rocket and purslane are very easy to grow, even in a window-box. They are especially rewarding as they continue to flourish as you cut from them. Sow from April onwards. Buy several packets of seeds at once because, although later sowings can be made, many shops have an annoying policy of selling the seeds only for a limited period from about March to May.

WALNUT DRESSING

Place two tablespoons of WALNUT OIL, three-quarters of a tablespoon of white wine VINEGAR and a little freshly ground black pepper in a clean screw-top jar and shake well.

HAZELNUT AND GOAT'S CHEESE SALAD

Make a mixed green salad of two types of LETTUCE, LAMB'S LETTUCE and RED CHICORY. Under the grill, toast 2–3 oz/50–75g HAZELNUTS in their skins until golden brown and irresistibly delicious – don't burn them. Warm a little goat's cheese in the microwave on Medium for 30 seconds. Add the nuts to the salad with the crumbled cheese, and toss in Hazelnut Dressing (below).

HAZELNUT DRESSING

Place two tablespoons of HAZELNUT OIL, three-quarters of a tablespoon of white wine VINEGAR and a little freshly ground black pepper in a clean screw-top jar and shake well.

VEGETARIAN SCOTCH EGG AND TOMATO

Home-made Scotch Eggs (see the vegetarian recipe on page 106) are delicious fresh from the oven. I make them in the oven rather than deep-frying them to cut down on fat and calorie content. Place the quartered, warm Scotch Egg on top of a bed of washed and trimmed WATERCRESS, CARROT cut into curls using a vegetable peeler or cheese plane, sliced CUCUMBER and diced CELERY. Spoon over warm Tomato Sauce (below).

TOMATO SAUCE

In a covered pan, sweat a small diced ONION and two large ripe TOMATOES, roughly chopped, with half a teaspoonful of ground CUMIN and CORIANDER and a crushed GARLIC clove, for about 10 minutes until soft. Remove from heat and blend in the liquidizer.

SPINACH AND BACON SALAD

Shred some freshly washed and dried SPINACH leaves into a serving bowl with two sticks of diced CELERY. Slice half an AVOCADO and turn the slices in a tablespoonful of LEMON JUICE (to prevent discolouring) before adding to the spinach. Grill two rashers of back BACON until crispy and browned. Using kitchen scissors, cut the bacon into small pieces over the top of the avocado and spinach. Toss on some warm Croutons (below) and sprinkle the whole with a tablespoonful of freshly grated PARMESAN CHEESE.

CROUTONS

Cube a slice of WHOLEMEAL BREAD. Lightly brush a pan with olive oil, and rub a cut clove of GARLIC round it. (Keep a frying-pan specifically for use where a garlic flavour doesn't matter. In other words, don't make your Crêpes Suzette in it!) Fry the croutons until golden brown. If you don't want to use oil because it is high in calories, 'toast' the croutons in a heavy-based pan over a moderate heat without the addition of oil.

CHICKEN TIKKA

Many major multiples and delicatessens now sell prepared CHICKEN TIKKA which you can cook in the oven or microwave according to the instructions on the pack. Chicken tikka makes an excellent warm salad. Serve it on a bed of LETTUCE, RADICCHIO, WATERCRESS, sliced CUCUMBER and a peeled and sliced ORANGE, tossed in Orange Dressing (overleaf).

ORANGE DRESSING

Place two tablespoons of SUNFLOWER, corn or soya OIL, the juice of half an ORANGE, half a tablespoonful of white wine VINEGAR and a little freshly ground black pepper in a clean screw-top jar and shake well.

If you have stopped buying chicken tikka from the supermarket since reports of an increased incidence of salmonella and *listeria monocytogenes* in chilled recipe dishes, try the recipe below:

TIKKA DRUMSTICKS

This dish should be marinated overnight if possible. Skin a couple of CHICKEN DRUMSTICKS and place in a dish suitable for marinating. Mix together the marinade: half a tub of strained GREEK YOGHURT, the juice of half a LEMON, a crushed clove of GARLIC, a small amount of grated ROOT GINGER and a pinch of SAFFRON strands (turmeric being an alternative, but not as nice). Pour the marinade over the drumsticks. Cover the dish and refrigerate. When you are ready to cook the dish, lightly dry-roast in a hot pan (i.e. a cast-iron frying-pan) a teaspoonful each of crushed CUMIN SEEDS, whole WHITE MUSTARD SEEDS and FENNEL SEEDS. Stir these into the marinade with a teaspoonful of GROUND CORIANDER and then transfer chicken and marinade to a baking dish. Cover and bake for 45 minutes at 375°F/190°C/Gas 5. Uncover and bake for a further 12–15 minutes, then eat hot. Left to cool, this sets beautifully and is ideal for picnics or portable meals.

CHICKEN LIVER AND
GREEN BEAN SALAD

Blanch 4 oz/100g GREEN BEANS (French or Bobby), and cut into bite-size pieces. Put on one side while you dice about 4 oz/100g CHICKEN LIVERS and heat ½ oz/15g unsalted BUTTER in a pan with a small clove of crushed GARLIC. Cook the livers very lightly so they remain pink in the middle. Remove the pan from the heat. Slice three SPRING ONIONS, add them together with the beans, to the cooked livers and stir well. Serve immediately.

If you have stopped cooking chicken products lightly since reports of an increased incidence of salmonella, then wait until you are again confident before trying the recipe rather than spoil the dish by overcooking the liver. Have something else today . . .

BARBARY DUCK BREAST SALAD

Duck-breast portions are conveniently sold by super-markets, butchers and poulterers. In my experience, Barbary ones are usually leaner, with the best flavour. Marinate one DUCK BREAST (with the skin on) for at least 4 hours in fresh ORANGE JUICE, naturally brewed SOY SAUCE, a little grated ROOT GINGER and – if you like – a finely diced green CHILLI. Remove from the marinade and put under a hot grill for 3 to 4 minutes either side. Meanwhile heat the marinade in a pan and reduce slightly. To serve, cut off the skin and fat from the duck breast and slice thinly. Arrange on a SALAD of green leaves, sliced SPRING ONIONS and thin slivers of ORANGE segments. Spoon over the marinade (or, if you prefer, a salad dressing of your choice).

Snack Suppers
(and all about Pizza)

There is nothing to stop you enjoying any of the other meals or dishes in *All for One* as a snack supper, but the recipes below are listed together because they are all especially light and therefore suitable for days when you have had a business lunch, or other large meal, and want only a snack in the evening.

VEGETABLES WITH YOGHURT 'MAYONNAISE' DIP

Instead of the usual all-raw *crudités*, try a combination of cooked vegetables, such as small ASPARAGUS spears and BROCCOLI florets, and crunchy raw RADICCHIO, PEPPERS and FENNEL. Dip into a creamy mix of equal parts of strained GREEK YOGHURT and very low fat NATURAL YOGHURT. You will probably need only the equivalent, in total, of a small pot of yoghurt – about 4–5 oz/100–150g. Add a free-range EGG yolk, season with sea salt and freshly ground black pepper to taste, and choose from the following flavourings: freshly chopped chives or dill, a teaspoonful of ready-made mustard, flaked and ground smoked fish, Indian spices in the form of pastes (such as Sharwood's) which blend in easily, and lemon juice and zest.

CAESAR SALAD DIP

A very tasty dip for *crudités*. Pound the contents of a small can of ANCHOVIES and a clove of GARLIC to a paste, using a pestle and mortar, then add two tablespoons of olive oil. Lightly beat in a free-range EGG yolk, add to the mixture, and then stir in 1 oz/25g freshly grated PARMESAN CHEESE. Dip in with FENNEL, CUCUMBER, PEPPERS, CARROTS, RADICCHIO – in fact any of your favourite raw vegetables, cut into bite-size pieces.

GOAT'S CHEESE AND
PEACH PARCELS

This is a neat little idea from Food and Wine from France, an organization which promotes French produce, for a delicious combination of cheese and fruit wrapped in a parcel of FILO PASTRY (strudel leaves). You will need two sheets of pastry and a ripe PEACH, peeled, halved and stoned. Cut the pastry into eight 7"/18cm squares and put one of these on a baking-sheet, brush it sparingly with a little melted unsalted BUTTER (½ oz/15g will be enough) and arrange another square on top so that the points cross the straight edges to form a star. Repeat until you have two lots of four layers. Place an individual chèvre (GOAT'S CHEESE), or a thin slice cut from a goat's cheese log or roll, on each of the filo 'stars' and top with an upturned peach half. Pull up the edges of the pastry and pinch together to seal the filling in a little 'money-bag' or purse. Brush with butter and bake for about 12 minutes at 375°F/190°C/Gas 5. Serve with a WATERCRESS salad.

CHEESE AND BISCUITS

You don't need to be told how to assemble cheese and biscuits . . . but I will just mention that cheese is, of course, high in fat, so make the cheese incidental and enjoy lots of fruit. Pears and grapes go especially well with it, or tasty wholemeal biscuits or oatcakes. Celery is still a favourite. Old-fashioned white celery has the most taste – the type sold with soil still around the base. Unfortunately it is less common nowadays and only available at a few greengrocers. The majority is now the self-blanching or green celery sold in polythene sleeves.

If you are interested in calories, hard and cream cheeses contain about 100–120 calories per oz/25g (130 calories for some blue cheeses). Brie, Camembert and Edam are slightly lower in calories: around 98.

STUFFED TOMATO

Slice the top from a large BEEFSTEAK TOMATO and cut out the pips and centre core – a serrated grapefruit knife makes quick work of this. Turn upside down to drain. Mix together enough COTTAGE CHEESE and either TUNA or smoked mackerel to fill the tomato, and season with LEMON JUICE and black pepper. Serve with slices of PUMPERNICKEL BREAD.

SCRAMBLED EGGS AND SMOKED SALMON

Lightly beat two free-range EGGS in a small jug with a little black pepper, a tablespoonful of SKIMMED MILK and a teaspoonful of chopped CHIVES (optional). Melt ½ oz/15g unsalted BUTTER in a saucepan and add the eggs, stirring all the time until creamy and set. Remove from the heat and stir in 2 oz/50g finely chopped SMOKED SALMON. You can scramble eggs without the addition of fat if you use a non-stick pan.

In the microwave: follow the manufacturer's instructions, but as a general rule (or if you've lost the book!) use Medium power because Full power tends to make the liquid separate out and the eggs hard and rubbery. Stir in the salmon for the last 20 seconds of cooking.

OLIVE BREAD

Whether French or Italian, crusty round loaves of yellowy olive bread tinted by the addition of olive oil and whole green olives in the dough, is absolutely delicious and very more-ish. Break off hunks, or cut genteelly thin slices, and enjoy with slivers of Parma, prosciutto, *jamón serrano* or other delicious Italian or Spanish HAM. Or why not serve it with slivers of SMOKED VENISON, SMOKED CHICKEN or SMOKED QUAIL?

Pizza and Focaccia Bread

While speaking of Italian bread, we mustn't forget focaccia. If you have an Italian delicatessen nearby it may well sell home-made pizza and focaccia, a simple flattish bread made with a little olive oil. Sometimes chopped bacon, prosciutto or herbs are added to the dough. Slit the bread and stuff with SEAFOOD SALAD, ARTICHOKE HEARTS, or MOZZARELLA SALAD, rather like a very hearty pitta.

Pizzas

Obviously, for a snack you are not going to roll up your sleeves and start making bread, but you can make your own focaccia or pizza dough and freeze it for later use.

Pizza dough

For a single pizza: 4 oz/100g each plain white UNBLEACHED and WHOLEMEAL FLOUR, and ¼ pint/150ml lukewarm water. Dissolve ½ oz/15g FRESH YEAST (or a ¼ oz/7g sachet of dried or fast-acting yeast) in the water. Sift the flour into a mixing-bowl and add a pinch of sea salt. Pour in the dissolved yeast and mix with a fork, then knead on a floured surface (or in the food processor with a dough-hook) for 3 to 5 minutes. Return the dough to the bowl and leave covered in a warm place for 20 minutes. Knock back the dough and knead lightly once again. Roll out to fit a pizza dish, or make a 9"/23cm circle on a lightly oiled baking-sheet. Now cover with a topping and bake, or freeze the base at this stage if you are completing the pizza later on.

Toppings

(You can also use these on French bread and *baguettes* for a 'cheats' pizza.)

Stage one

You can achieve a very good flavour and crispy edges to the dough by brushing the top of the pizza with a mixture of olive oil, crushed GARLIC and chopped fresh HERBS such as basil, oregano, marjoram and tarragon. The addition of a little TOMATO PURÉE is optional. You can also spread pesto as a topping, but personally I think it too sweet.

Stage two

Now add the topping, such as

- *quattro formaggi* – four types of CHEESE, such as Mozzarella, Dolcelatte, Parmesan (though this is best put on after cooking) and Emmental
- ANCHOVY FILLETS, OLIVES, sliced TOMATOES (fresh or dried), ARTICHOKE HEARTS and red PEPPERS
- PEPPERONI or salami, MUSHROOMS, TOMATOES, CAPERS and ONIONS.

Baking

Cook pizza at 400°F/200°C/Gas 6 for up to 25 minutes, depending on topping.

FOCACCIA

Make a quantity of basic pizza dough (above) and when kneading for the last time add some trimmed and diced BACON or prosciutto, or even a small amount of PEPPERONI or salami. Roll out to fit a Swiss-roll tin and brush with oil. Bake at 400°F/200°C/Gas 6 for 15 minutes.

OLIVES

Incidentally, if you like olives some of the most delicious can be obtained from Justin de Blank Provisions. They are all unstoned, and come from Le Moulin de Daudet, Fontvieille, near Arles. There are French green olives marinated in lemon brine with added thyme and rosemary, and Italian black olives marinated in oil, thyme and rosemary. Justin de Blank also provide tiny Spanish *coquillos* olives that are delicious with fish. Once you have opened the can of olives, transfer the contents to a non-metallic container, cover and put in the fridge where they will keep well for up to a fortnight.

SMOKED TROUT

Probably more than a snack, but then I suppose it rather depends how much you are going to eat . . . either a whole trout . . . or half . . . or even a small fillet. Enjoy it in traditional style with wedges of LEMON, freshly ground black pepper and brown BREAD and BUTTER. Or arrange pieces of trout with slices of juicy PEAR alongside a small salad of LAMB'S LETTUCE and ROCKET or watercress, both of which have some bite to stand up to the flavour of the smoked fish.

DATES AND BACON

Stone some fresh DATES and cut in half. Flatten a couple of rashers of smoked back BACON and cut into pieces large enough to wrap round the dates. Impale the wrapped dates on a wooden skewer which will hold them all together and keep the bacon in place. Grill under a moderate heat, turning occasionally, until the bacon is crisp.

CAMBOZOLA ON TOAST

Cut the rind off about 2–3 oz/50–75g CAMBOZOLA or other ripe, soft blue cheese and beat with a level tablespoonful of *FROMAGE FRAIS* or quark, a teaspoonful of LEMON JUICE, and some freshly ground black pepper. Toast some thick slices of French or rye BREAD on one side. Then spread the other sides with the cheese mixture and place under a moderate (not too hot) grill or in a hot oven until the cheese melts. Serve with GRAPES and/or a green SALAD. You can also use the spread on Crisprolls or French Toasts.

PARMA HAM AND FRUIT

Thin slices of PARMA HAM eaten with a delicious BREAD such as *Pain Poîlane* and juicy FRUIT make a delicious and low-calorie supper or light meal. Some fruit to try: Asian pears, mangoes, pawpaws, figs, lychees and grapes. With a good bread you don't really need any butter.

PAWPAW AND PARMA HAM

Halve a nice ripe PAWPAW (also called papaya), scoop out the black seeds and peel it. Cut the flesh into chunks or slices and dip them in freshly squeezed LIME JUICE. Wrap them in PARMA HAM to make little parcels.

SEAFOOD AND AÏOLI

Choose one of your favourite SHELLFISH for this dish, or make up a selection from ready-cooked whole prawns, langoustines, crab claws, or whatever is available. Then make that delicious, thick garlic mayonnaise: aïoli. Crush four cloves of GARLIC and a pinch of sea salt in a mortar. Put into a bowl and blend in a free-range EGG yolk. Now slowly add the OLIVE OIL, a drop at a time to start with and then gradually a thin drizzle until you have incorporated about ¼ pint/150ml. As you work, the aïoli will become thick and firm. Season with more salt, if needed, freshly ground black pepper and a little LEMON JUICE.

PAN BAGNAT

Make a meal of a 'sandwich' with a PAN BAGNAT from Provence. You can assemble one yourself. You will need a crusty round LOAF or roll which you should split in half. If the bread is thick, pull out some of the inside to make more room for the filling! Crush a clove of GARLIC in a tablespoonful or two of olive oil and brush the inside of the 'sandwich' with this mixture. Fill with crunchy LETTUCE such as batavia (escarole), slices of RED and GREEN PEPPERS, ONION, hard-boiled free-range EGG, ANCHOVY FILLETS, BLACK OLIVES, ripe TOMATOES and chopped PARSLEY. Close your eyes and bite in, to be transported to Juan les Pins, Antibes and sun and fun – but without the sand in your *pan bagnat*!

OPEN SANDWICHES

Slices of dark rye bread
or pumpernickel
or crispbread
or Crisprolls
– all delicious topped with colourful combinations such as

- rare roast beef with horseradish sauce
- smoked chicken topped with sliced green olives stuffed with anchovies
- slices of Edam topped with orange segments
- Boursin topped with sliced cherry tomatoes
- slices of free-range hard-boiled egg topped with anchovy fillets
- large prawns on mayonnaise – serve with a wedge of lemon
- dill (pickled herring available in cans and jars) with sliced hard-boiled free-range egg and cress
- smoked salmon with lemon juice and black pepper
- thin slices of pear with even thinner slices of prosciutto ham
- taramosalata (home-made, see below) topped with olives
- black olive spread or pâté (from delicatessen)
- asparagus tips with crispy bacon pieces
- ripe blue Stilton or Roquefort topped with chopped walnuts
- peanut butter topped with slices of banana
- clotted cream topped with sliced figs.

POÎLANE BREAD

Pain Poîlane from Paris is the most delicious chewy ... crusty ... aerated ... sourdough rye bread. Toast it lightly and top it at once with CAMBOZOLA CHEESE and slices of ripe Victoria PLUMS (or cherry tomatoes for the less adventurous).

TARAMOSALATA

A little SMOKED COD'S ROE goes a long way (but this recipe freezes and keeps well in the fridge if the cheese has a long shelf-life). Place about 2 oz/50g roe in a liquidizer and blend with juice of 1 SMALL LEMON, 1 oz/25g FRESH WHOLEMEAL BREAD-CRUMBS and 2–3 oz/50–75g QUARK or similar low fat soft white cheese which I use instead of high calorie oil or butter. Eat with crudités, on toast, in sandwiches, etc.

Soups

CUCUMBER AND WALNUT SOUP

This is an 'instant' cold soup, ideal for summer. To make enough for one, finely dice a third of a small unpeeled CUCUMBER. The diced cucumber gives the soup some texture, and the peel adds colour (and fibre!), but you can peel the cucumber and liquidize it if you prefer. Lightly grill, or gently brown in a pan using dry heat, 1½–2 oz/40–50g WALNUT PIECES, then crush them using a pestle and mortar. Add them to the cucumber, stir in two tablespoons of SOURED CREAM or *crème fraîche*, and about ¼ pint/150ml cultured BUTTERMILK or very thin drinking yoghurt. Season to taste with sea salt, freshly ground black pepper and chopped CHIVES.

WATERCRESS SOUP

Delicious, and something of a classic, either hot or cold. Wash a bunch of WATERCRESS and remove any woody stalks or roots, but leave in most of the finer stalks. Scrub a medium-sized POTATO and dice. Place the watercress and potato in a pan with ½ pint/300ml VEGETABLE STOCK and simmer, covered, for 15–20 minutes. Cool slightly, then liquidize. Season to taste. If serving hot, return to the pan to heat through. If serving cold, you could stir in a few tablespoons of NATURAL YOGHURT or cultured buttermilk before serving. This adds body and a pleasant tart creaminess.

POTATO AND RAW VEGETABLE SOUP

Raw vegetable soups are true vitality food. This simple recipe with a spicy flavour was given to me by Dame Beryl Grey. It makes gallons, but you can scale it down, freeze some for later, or live on it for a week! Scrub 1 lb/450g POTATOES and put them on to boil. Meanwhile wash and chop a LEEK and a bunch of WATERCRESS and put ready in the food processor. Add a grated organic CARROT and a tablespoonful of chopped PARSLEY, some chopped MINT leaves, a 14 oz/400g can of TOMATOES and 1 pint/600ml VEGETABLE STOCK. By now the potatoes should be cooked, so drain and add them to the ingredients in the food processor and blend all to a purée. Enjoy hot or cold (although if you heat it up it is no longer a raw vegetable soup!).

GREEN CHICKEN SOUP!

When I interviewed Fenella Fielding for *Here's Health* magazine, she gave me a terrific soup recipe and advised me to make friends with my butcher so that he would give me lots of chicken feet to make stock for it. I must own up to not always making chicken-feet stock, but I do like the soup.

For a complete meal for one, you will need a skinned and boned CHICKEN BREAST. Shred the meat into ¾ pint/450ml strong CHICKEN STOCK and simmer for 20 minutes. While the chicken is cooking, hard-boil a free-range EGG; when cool, shell and finely chop. Stir into the stock a tablespoonful of naturally brewed SOY SAUCE, three sliced SPRING ONIONS and a little freshly ground black pepper. Continue simmering the soup while you wash and finely chop a small bunch of WATERCRESS. Add this to the pan and cook for a further 3–4 minutes. Sprinkle the egg into the serving bowl and ladle the soup over it.

BACON AND PASTA SOUP

Sometimes this turns out more like a pasta dish proper than a soup, depending on the amount of liquid used. Dice one or two rashers of BACON and an ONION, add a clove of GARLIC and a CELERY stick, and sauté all together in a little olive oil. Remove from the heat and add a couple of chopped ripe TOMATOES (or a small can – 7 oz/200g), plus about ½ pint/300ml VEGETABLE STOCK. Bring to the boil, add a handful of WHOLEMEAL MACARONI and cook for about 12 minutes or until the macaroni is *al dente*. Stir in a scrubbed and grated organic CARROT and/or some freshly chopped PARSLEY. Heat through quickly, but leave the carrot and parsley crunchy.

CARROT AND LENTIL SOUP

Dice an ONION and crush a clove of GARLIC, and sauté them in a little olive oil until soft. Scrub and dice two organic CARROTS and add them to the pan. Continue cooking for 2–3 minutes. Pick over about 2 oz/50g RED LENTILS and wash them before adding to the pan with ¾ pint/450ml VEGETABLE STOCK. Cover, and simmer for about 30 minutes until the lentils are tender. Season to taste with sea salt and freshly ground black pepper. You can liquidize the soup if you like it smooth, or leave it so that all the various ingredients are visible. It's nice to stir in a dessertspoonful of chopped CORIANDER or chervil leaves just before serving.

CARIBBEAN CHOWDER

Sweat a small diced ONION, a GREEN CHILLI, about a third of a GREEN PEPPER, four or five sliced OKRA, a crushed clove of GARLIC and a small quantity of grated ROOT GINGER in a saucepan with a little olive oil for about 5 minutes. Cube a small amount (about 3–4 oz/75–100g) of skinned and filleted WHITE FISH – a cheap one like coley is fine for this soup – and add to the pan together with a handful of shelled North Atlantic PRAWNS. Season with freshly ground black pepper and a pinch of PAPRIKA. Add just over ½ pint/300ml FISH or VEGETABLE STOCK and a small can of TOMATOES (7 oz/200g). Cover and cook for about 15 minutes, then stir in a handful of frozen SWEETCORN kernels and cook for a further 5 minutes.

RED PEPPER AND TOMATO

Pressure cookers make excellent soup, and very quickly. For this soup deseed and roughly chop a RED PEPPER and place it in the cooker with a roughly chopped POTATO, CARROT, 4 RIPE TOMATOES and ¼ pint/150ml water. Bring to full pressure and cook for six minutes. Liquidize the contents of the pan, adding boiling water if you like the soup thinner, and season to taste. An equally delicious combination is YELLOW PEPPER and CARROT without the tomato.

Mainly
Vegetarian

VEGETARIAN SCOTCH EGGS

Unless you have a small oven (such as a combination microwave oven) you will probably not want to bake just one Scotch Egg. The quantities I suggest will make two. In case you thought I had got it wrong when I said 'bake' rather than the usual 'deep-fry', I meant just that because baking cuts down on fat and gives just as good results.

First hard-boil two free-range EGGS and while they are cooking prepare the coating. Grate an ONION and about 2 oz/50g each of WHOLEMEAL BREADCRUMBS and ground NUTS (for example, brazils, walnuts, almonds) of your choice. Mix the onion, nuts and crumbs in a bowl and bind with about half a tablespoon each of olive oil and TOMATO KETCHUP. Add seasoning and some freshly chopped PARSLEY. Mix with a little boiling water to make a stiff paste and form this around the shelled eggs. Bake in a moderate oven (350°F/180°C/Gas 4) for about 20 minutes, turning once.

SPICED EGGS AND CAULIFLOWER

This is a dish of cauliflower cooked with Indian spices in a yoghurt sauce to which you add hard-boiled quail eggs (or standard free-range if quail eggs are unavailable). So first hard-boil the QUAIL EGGS – about four will be enough and they will take 3 minutes. Wash and cut about half a small CAULIFLOWER into florets, and top and tail 2–3 oz/50–75g GREEN BEANS. Heat a tablespoonful of olive oil and sauté a little freshly grated ROOT GINGER, CUMIN SEEDS, BLACK MUSTARD SEEDS and a very small quantity of GROUND TURMERIC – cover the pan, as they pop about! Now add the cauliflower and beans and fry for a couple of minutes to brown the cauliflower, remove from the heat and pour in a wineglassful of VEGETABLE STOCK. Cover, and cook for about 10 minutes, stirring from time to time. Again remove from the heat and stir in a small pot of NATURAL YOGHURT. Transfer to a serving dish and drop the shelled quail eggs into the sauce.

NUT RISSOLES

Nut rissoles sound depressingly awful, but really this particular combination of brown lentils and nuts is very pleasant. The quantities given here will make four rissoles. First wash 2 oz/50g BROWN LENTILS and boil them for about 30 minutes until they are soft. Meanwhile toast 1 oz/25g WHOLEMEAL BREADCRUMBS for the coating. Then grate a small peeled ONION into a bowl and stir in 3 oz/75g ground or finely chopped CASHEW NUTS, or a mixture of cashews and Brazils. Add a little chopped PARSLEY and season to taste with sea salt and freshly ground black pepper. Add the drained lentils, stir well, and form the mixture into rissoles. Roll them in the breadcrumbs and gently fry in a little VEGETABLE OIL for about 6 or 7 minutes on each side. Serve with POTATOES and a GREEN VEGETABLE.

EASTERN CHICKPEAS AND AUBERGINE

Cube a large AUBERGINE and place in a colander. Sprinkle with sea salt and leave for an hour to drain, then pat dry with absorbent kitchen paper. Heat a tablespoonful of olive oil and sauté a chopped GREEN CHILLI, a crushed clove of GARLIC and a teaspoonful of WHITE MUSTARD SEEDS. Stir in a little GROUND CUMIN and then add the aubergine and a couple of sliced small COURGETTES. You can make this pleasantly moist by adding a small can (7 oz/200g) of TOMATOES, drained, though it is fine without them. Cover and cook in its own steam for about 30 minutes, or longer if you like your aubergines very mushy. Stir in 3 oz/75g CHICKPEAS (canned or previously pressure-cooked) about 15 minutes before the end of cooking, and some freshly chopped CORIANDER LEAVES for the last couple of minutes before serving.

KIBBEH

A word or two of explanation about these Middle Eastern 'rissoles' that are shaped like large eggs. They are sometimes filled with spiced ground (minced) lamb, but this is a vegetarian version.

Soak 2 oz/50g of BULGUR (cracked wheat) for about 10 minutes in enough water to cover. Then mix with a finely diced CHILLI, a crushed clove of GARLIC, a small grated ONION and a tablespoonful of freshly chopped CORIANDER LEAVES. Make the filling in a separate bowl by mixing together 2 oz/50g very finely chopped, or ground, CASHEW NUTS, a tablespoonful of CURRANTS, a small grated CARROT and a pinch each of GROUND CINNAMON and NUTMEG. To assemble, take a handful of the bulgur mixture, roll into a ball and flatten it in your hand. Put a small amount of the filling in the middle and mould the bulgur mixture around it. Place the kibbeh on a lightly oiled baking sheet and bake at 375°F/190°C/Gas 5 for 25 minutes. You can also use hard-boiled quail eggs as the filling to make 'Scotched' quail eggs. Vary the spices, and you have curried, rather than Middle Eastern, quail eggs!

CHEESE AND ONION PANCAKES

Make a pancake batter by sifting 1½ oz/40g plain WHOLEMEAL (or white) FLOUR into a bowl with a pinch of sea salt. Add half a beaten free-range EGG and enough SKIMMED MILK to make a batter the consistency of single cream. Stir in half a grated ONION and 1 oz/25g of a well-flavoured CHEESE such as Gruyère or mature Cheddar.

To make the pancakes, heat a small amount of VEGETABLE OIL in a frying-pan and then add tablespoons of the batter mixture. Cook for about a minute and then turn the little pancakes and cook the other sides. Serve hot. Nice with Fried Almonds and Spinach (below).

FRIED ALMONDS AND SPINACH

Wash some young leaves of SPINACH or lamb's lettuce (about 6 oz/175g) and drain well, then chop roughly. Sauté a crushed clove of GARLIC in a little olive oil or unsalted butter and add a tablespoonful of FLAKED ALMONDS to brown. Add the spinach and cook, stirring constantly, for 2 minutes. Sprinkle with a little naturally brewed SOY SAUCE and serve.

TORTILLA

Tortilla is served hot or cold as a *tapas* snack in Spain and it is a favourite with those who like omelettes. You need a small dish of cold cooked POTATOES, preferably waxy ones like La Ratte (cornichon) or another salad potato, although Maris Piper will do well. Dice the potatoes and gently heat a little olive oil in an omelette pan. Beat two large free-range EGGS until frothy and season with sea salt and freshly ground black pepper or a pinch of paprika. Put the diced potato into the pan, heat through, then pour in the beaten eggs. Stir the mixture around with a wooden spoon until the egg is nearly set, then drop in 4 or 5 stoned GREEN OLIVES. Ease the edges of the omelette away from the pan to neaten them and leave to cook for a few moments until as soft or firm as you like it. Serve immediately.

BOREK (STUFFED PASTRIES)

These Turkish pastries are simple to make and very tasty. They are filled with sheep's milk cheese and parsley – it's quite surprising how generous Turkish cooking is with parsley. All you need is a couple of sheets of FILO PASTRY (strudel leaves, or *yufka* in Turkish) which you can cut into large squares (about 6″ × 6″ or 15 × 15cm). Mix together some tangy SHEEP'S MILK (or goat's milk) CHEESE with lots of freshly chopped PARSLEY, some freshly ground pepper and a little LEMON JUICE. Roll the cheese up in the pastry to make cigar shapes, or fold into triangles. Brush lightly with melted BUTTER, which will also help to seal the edges, and bake for 12–15 minutes in a moderate oven (about 375°F/190°C/ Gas 5). If you're feeling reckless, deep-fry them and pat off excess fat with absorbent kitchen paper. Experiment with other filling ingredients such as pine kernels, ricotta cheese, chopped spinach, or currants.

RICE AND BEAN SALAD

A variation on the Caribbean theme of rice 'n' peas. I pressure-cook brown rice because it's so quick and it gives good results. So many people cannot resist stirring rice while it is cooking – this results in a sticky, starchy mass at the end of cooking. If you use a pressure cooker you can't stir it, so the grains remain individual and fluffy – provided you don't overcook them.

Mix the cooked BROWN RICE (about 2 oz/50g dry weight per person, if you are starting from scratch), drained if necessary, with an individual portion of: cooked KIDNEY BEANS (either canned or pressure-cooked while you are cooking the rice), or diced smoked tofu, or vegetarian frankfurters. Then add some diced GREEN PEPPERS and SPRING ONIONS, and serve while warm.

FRENCH BUTTER BEANS

Sauté a diced ONION and a small TURNIP in a saucepan, then add about ¾ pint/450ml MUSHROOM SOUP (packet soup-mix will do) and a small can (7 oz/200g) of BUTTER BEANS, drained. Bring to the boil, then reduce to just below simmering point while you prepare a bread 'lid'.

Cut 2–3 thick slices from a *BAGUETTE*. Make some garlic butter by crushing a clove of GARLIC and mashing it with 1–1½ oz/ 25–40g unsalted BUTTER. Stir in a teaspoonful of ready-made WHOLE-GRAIN MUSTARD and spread on one side of each slice of bread. Make a 'lid' for the butter beans in the pan with the bread, spread sides uppermost, continue cooking on the hob for about 10 minutes, then pop under the grill to crisp the top of the bread; or transfer the beans to an ovenproof dish, top with the bread, then put into a moderate oven for 10–15 minutes.

ROSTI

Swiss fried potatoes are usually served as a vegetable accompaniment, but they can be a dish in their own right on certain occasions. I like to make them with raw potatoes – use either new or old. Scrub or peel 8 oz/225g POTATOES and grate them (quickly done in a food processor). Remove excess moisture by wrapping the grated potato in a tea-towel and squeezing. Season – at this stage you can also stir in chives, onion, garlic or cheese, if you like. Melt some BUTTER mixed with vegetable oil in a frying-pan and add the potato, pressing down well to form a large 'cake' and neatening the edges with a spatula. Cook on one side for 10 minutes until brown, then carefully turn and cook the other side. Serve at once.

Fruit Salads, Other Puddings

(and Quick Comforters)

Wherever Greek yoghurt is used in these recipes you can substitute (depending on your position in the cholesterol stakes):

- clotted, double, whipping or single cream
- *crème fraîche* or soured cream
- *fromage blanc* or *fromage frais*
- natural yoghurt.

Fruit salads

FRUIT SALAD

You don't really need me to tell you how to make a fruit salad as you have probably often washed and chopped or diced fruit in your favourite combinations. But do try adding it to a fruit-juice base, such as apple or orange, rather than a sugar syrup. As long as the fruit is fresh and not discoloured all fruit salads look appetizing and attractive, but you can play around with colour themes; for example, use all greenish fruits, all yellow and orange ones, or all red ones, or make attractive combinations such as green and yellow/orange.

HOT FRUIT SALAD

Make as much as you like, because this is equally delicious for breakfast and will keep in the fridge for five days. Take about 2 oz/50g each of DRIED PEARS and PEACHES and put into a microwave dish with enough hot water to cover, a stick of CINNAMON, one CLOVE and the juice of half a LEMON. Cook on Moderate heat until the fruit is plump and softened. Meanwhile peel and core an APPLE and a firm PEAR and cut into chunks. Add these, with a handful of Australian SEEDED RAISINS and a grating of NUTMEG, to the dried fruit and continue to cook in the microwave until the apple and pear are tender.

SUMMER FRUIT-SALAD TARTLETS

Most fruit tartlets are made of rich pastry (*pâte sucrée*) bases filled with a layer of confectioner's custard and topped with glazed fresh fruit. You are, of course, free to follow this example, but for occasions when you want a much quicker and less fattening fruit tartlet, make some filo pastry (strudel leaf) cases as outlined in the Salmon Tartlet recipe (page 42). Fill with sliced STRAWBERRIES, FIGS and MANGO, and whole BLACKCURRANTS, REDCURRANTS, CHERRIES and RASPBERRIES.

If you want to glaze the tartlets, make a glaze or gel with fruit juice and a setting agent such as gelatine, agar-agar (a vegetarian seaweed alternative), or Gelozone (a brand of vegetarian setting agent). Choose a fruit juice that matches the fruit in colour or flavour, and follow the instructions for the particular setting agent. (If you are in doubt, or if there are no instructions, the table on page 123 will act as a guide.)

FRUIT KEBABS

Delightful in summer, when you can arrange on a wooden skewer a variety of STRAWBERRIES and other large berries such as TAYBERRIES, stoned CHERRIES, halved APRICOTS, slices of PEACH or nectarine, whole GRAPES, fresh DATES, pieces of MELON, chunks of PINEAPPLE, PLUM halves and, if you like them, slices of CHINESE GOOSEBERRY. When fresh fruit is scarce, soaked, or no-need-to-soak DRIED FRUITS such as peaches, pears, apricots and prunes will also add colour and flavour.

PAWPAW SALAD

Halve the pawpaw (papaya) and remove the black seeds. Sprinkle with LIME (or lemon) JUICE and fill with fresh STRAWBERRIES.

Other puddings

SPICED FRESH CHERRY YOGHURT

Wash and stone 12 oz/350g ripe CHERRIES and liquidize 2–3 oz/50–75g of them with about 4 oz/100g GREEK YOGHURT and a small pinch each of grated NUTMEG, CLOVES and CINNAMON. Put the purée in a serving dish and arrange the remaining cherries, halved, on top.

MERINGUE MELBA

Fill a MERINGUE NEST with slices of fresh PEACH (if you don't use it all, keep the remainder for tomorrow's breakfast cereal!), fresh or defrosted RASPBERRIES and a scoop of dairy or Cornish VANILLA ICE-CREAM.

STRAWBERRY SHORTCAKE

Spread a round or petticoat-tail SHORTBREAD with thick, creamy GREEK YOGHURT and top with sliced fresh STRAWBERRIES.

FRUIT BRÛLÉE

Stew or microwave a single portion (4–6 oz/100–175g) of a fruit such as BLACKCURRANTS, RHUBARB or GOOSEBERRIES and then sweeten to taste. Place in an individual ramekin and top with two tablespoons of GREEK YOGHURT. Sprinkle with two teaspoons of DEMERARA SUGAR and grill until the sugar is bubbling. Cool, eat and enjoy!

FRUIT FOOLS

Cold cooked fruits such as GOOSEBERRIES, BLACKCURRANTS and APPLES, or dried fruits (PRUNES and APRICOTS, for instance), can be mixed with GREEK YOGHURT to make fruit fools. Uncooked soft fruits like STRAWBERRIES and RASPBERRIES are also suitable,

and so is MANGO. Sweeten to taste with a little CLEAR HONEY –
although many fruits are sweet enough without, especially when
mixed with Greek yoghurt.

GRILLED PEACH

Halve and stone a PEACH and top with a mound of CURD
CHEESE (you will need about 2 oz/50g for each fruit) mixed with a
crushed DIGESTIVE BISCUIT, a drop of VANILLA ESSENCE and a few
chopped PISTACHIO NUTS. Grill until warmed through.

BROWN-BREAD ICE-CREAM
WITH APRICOTS

Liquidize a small can (7 oz/200g) of APRICOTS in fruit juice
and pour into a dessert glass. Top with a scoop of good-quality
BROWN-BREAD ICE-CREAM (or Cornish vanilla, if you prefer) and
drizzle over it a dessertspoonful of MAPLE SYRUP.

CARAMELIZED ORANGE

Grate some of the zest from a large, juicy organic ORANGE,
and then peel the fruit. Remove the pips, pith and membrane, slice
in thin rounds and arrange in a ramekin. Sprinkle with a teaspoonful of GRAND MARNIER (orange liqueur). Put 1½ oz/40g
BROWN SUGAR (such as demerara or muscovado) and two tablespoons of water in a heavy saucepan. Bring to the boil and continue
boiling for about 10 minutes (or cook in a microwave on High)
until golden brown. Dilute with up to the same volume of boiling
water and allow to cool, then pour the liquid over the orange and
sprinkle with the grated zest. If possible, leave to marinate for an
hour or so to bring out the flavour of the orange.

STRAWBERRIES WITH CRUNCHY AMARETTI CREAM

Wash and halve a small dish of STRAWBERRIES, leaving them un-hulled as you are going to dip them into a sauce. Mix 4 oz/100g GREEK YOGHURT with a little grated organic ORANGE rind and then stir in one or two finely crushed AMARETTI BISCUITS and a drop of ALMOND ESSENCE. Arrange the strawberries around the 'cream' and dip in.

RHUBARB AND STRAWBERRY COMPÔTE

Wash and slice three sticks of young, pink RHUBARB and put into a microwave dish with a lid. Add four tablespoons of REDCURRANT or red-grape JUICE and a pinch each of GROUND CINNAMON and MIXED SPICE. Microwave on Medium for 3–4 minutes, stirring once or twice, or stew the fruit gently in a saucepan. Remove and cool slightly while you hull and halve 4–6 oz/100–175g STRAWBERRIES. Mix the fruits together and serve with GREEK YOGHURT.

CREAMY ORANGE WITH MAPLE SYRUP

Peel and slice a large, juicy organic ORANGE, remove the pips. Place in a ramekin, spoon over some thick and creamy GREEK YOGHURT, then top with lashings of MAPLE SYRUP! If you can stand by in the face of such temptation, wait until the syrup has passed through the yoghurt to reach the orange slices.

FRUITY PANCAKES

Ready-made pancakes are a great standby. Use either home-made ones (see below) which can be frozen, or bought crêpes in vacuum packs. Top with freshly squeezed LEMON JUICE and

CLEAR HONEY (or maple syrup, or any other sweetener of your choice), or fill with fruit purée made from fresh or dried fruits. For quick results, plump dried fruit in the microwave in a little fruit juice and/or brandy or rum.

To make pancakes: Sift 4 oz/100g WHOLEMEAL FLOUR into a mixing bowl with a pinch of sea salt. Make a well in the centre and add a beaten free-range EGG with a little SKIMMED MILK. Using a fork and working from the centre, draw in the flour to make a stiff batter. Carefully and gently add enough milk (about ¼ pint/150ml in total) to make a batter the consistency of single cream.

To cook the pancakes, heat a little VEGETABLE OIL in an omelette pan and pour in about a tablespoonful of the batter mixture, tilting the pan so that the batter thinly covers the base. Cook until set and then flip over to cook the other side. Pancakes freeze well with a sheet of freezer paper between each one – in this way you can easily take one at a time from the freezer when required.

BUCKWHEAT CRÊPES

Instead of using wholemeal flour for your pancakes, try BUCKWHEAT FLOUR for a change. Instead of milk, the liquid added with the EGG should be half water and half CIDER or beer. These are traditional in Brittany, where they are accompanied by cider drunk out of special ceramic cups.

QUICK CRÊPES SUZETTE

Place a couple of cooked PANCAKES in a shallow non-stick pan, folding them in quarters. Squeeze over the juice of an ORANGE and half a LEMON and add a tablespoonful of GRAND MARNIER (orange liqueur) and half a tablespoonful of yellow GALIANO (optional). Heat through gently.

EASY-PEASY APPLE AND
GUAVA STRUDEL

This makes about six to eight portions, so unless you want to become a heavyweight entry in *The Guinness Book of Records* you are going to have to share this around or freeze some. That's not to say it's a high-calorie dessert – it isn't; it's just that alongside a bowl of thick, strained GREEK YOGHURT, it becomes irresistible.

Take three sheets of FILO PASTRY (strudel leaves). Peel and core two COOKING APPLES and a GUAVA (removing the pips from the guava) and cut the flesh into chunks. Place in a microwave dish with a lid, together with the juice of half a LEMON, two handfuls of Australian SEEDED RAISINS (seedless raisins are hopeless for this purpose), a CINNAMON STICK, a few whole ALLSPICE BERRIES and CLOVES, and a little water to prevent burning. Microwave gently on Low to Medium until the apple and guava are well softened – about 4–5 minutes.* Put the pastry on a pastry-board, melt very little (¼–½ oz/7–15g) unsalted BUTTER and brush this lightly between the layers of filo, leaving enough to brush the top. Place the apple filling in a long 'sausage' down the centre of the pastry, tuck in the ends of the filo, then brush the edges with butter and roll up the strudel. Brush the outside with the remaining butter and bake on High (400°F/200°C/Gas 6) for about 15 minutes until golden brown.

If you want to continue in your belief that this is a healthy dessert omit the finishing touch, which is to make a simple icing. Sift ICING SUGAR into a basin (the amount depends on how many slices you are going to finish in one sitting, so if you are freezing some portions ice them after they have defrosted and just before serving. About 4 oz/100g icing sugar takes around one table-spoonful of hot water). Stir in enough (i.e. very little) just-boiled water to make the icing; then add the secret ingredient – a drop of

---

* This can be done in a saucepan over a moderate heat, but it is difficult to keep the heat low enough to prevent the apple from becoming mushy and losing its shape as you stir to ensure even cooking.

BITTER ORANGE OIL (from Culpeper's, the herbalist) – and pour or spoon the icing over the strudel.

INSTANT TRIFLE

Drain a small can of APRICOT HALVES canned in fruit juice, and reserve the juice. Put some broken BOUDOIR BISCUITS (sponge fingers) in an individual ramekin or dessert glass and pour the juice over them. Place an apricot half on top of the soaked biscuits. Put the other apricot halves in a food processor with some GREEK YOGHURT and blend to a purée. Spoon the purée over the fruit and biscuits.

Quick comforters

I know we said in our little pep talk at the beginning of *All for One* that we would not be using food as a reward or emotional back-up, but if you are desperate for something sweet some of the following ideas might be as satisfying as and nutritionally a better investment than confectionery.

GRANOLA LAYER

Arrange some STEWED APPLE or sliced FRESH FRUIT in a dessert glass between layers of GRANOLA (crunchy breakfast cereal such as Jordan's Original Crunchy) and GREEK YOGHURT.

SALLY LUNN

Cut a SALLY LUNN (or other teacake or bun) in half horizontally, and toast. Spread with ½ oz/25g BUTTER into which you have worked a teaspoonful of GROUND CINNAMON.

Scone with Brandy Butter

Halve a WHOLEMEAL FRUIT SCONE and warm in the microwave on High for 20 seconds. Remove, and spread with BRANDY BUTTER.

Sweet Toasted Sandwich

Mix 4 oz/100g RICOTTA CHEESE with a teaspoonful of MUSCOVADO SUGAR and two teaspoons of CANDIED PEEL. Use as a filling for two slices of WHOLEMEAL BREAD in a toasted-sandwich-maker.

Dried Fruit Petits-Fours

Health books often recommend dried fruits as a substitute for sweets. Although they are still sweet and sticky and will be tut-tutted over by the dental hygienist, at least they contain a good proportion of fibre, with vitamins and minerals. These dried fruit sweets can also be used as *petits-fours*.

Put 2 oz/50g NUTS such as walnuts and/or almonds in a food processor together with 4 oz/100g DRIED FRUIT of your choice, for example apricots, dates (stoned of course!) or figs, and season with a pinch of GROUND CINNAMON, mixed spice, ground ginger or whatever other spice you prefer. Add a little (up to about a tablespoonful) of CLEAR HONEY to get the mixture to stick together, and whizz. Roll small (walnut-sized) balls of the mixture into shape – in *desiccated coconut*, or in carob or cocoa powder if you like – and place them in *petits-fours* paper cases. Store in an airtight tin.

Setting Agents
To set 1 pint/600ml fruit juice (or other liquid)

Use either a saucepan, or a jug in the microwave.

Gelatine	3 level teaspoons	Follow the directions on the packet. Sprinkle on to hot liquid and stir until dissolved. Or sprinkle on to cold and bring to the boil, stirring to dissolve.
Agar-agar	2 level teaspoons I find for mousse, soufflé, etc. this amount makes too firm a set and I usually use half to a third of this quantity of agar-agar.	Sprinkle on to cold water or other liquid before bringing to the boil, stirring, to dissolve. *Don't be tempted to sprinkle on to hot liquid as you might with gelatine – you will just create a coagulated lump.*
Gelozone	2 level teaspoons	Follow the directions on the packet: mix to a smooth paste with a little cold water. Add to the rest of the liquid. Bring to the boil and simmer for 2 minutes.

Left-overs

Left-overs are not very sexy, but then sometimes one finds oneself alone in the house with nothing but the cold comfort of a fridge full of left-overs. If that is the case, you have one's sympathy (hey-ho!) and some suggestions . . .

Cold potatoes

INDIAN POTATOES

Heat a heavy-based frying-pan and dry-roast some CUMIN SEEDS and BLACK MUSTARD SEEDS until they give off a delicious aroma and go pop. Heat a tablespoonful of CORN OIL in a saucepan and sauté a diced onion. When the onion is soft, add two chopped TOMATOES, a teaspoonful of GROUND CUMIN, the prepared seeds and the diced cold POTATO. Cook for about 10 minutes, stirring to prevent sticking. Remove from the heat and add a tablespoonful of freshly chopped CORIANDER LEAVES. Serve warm or cold.

POTATO AND BROAD BEAN SALAD

Strictly for cold NEW POTATOES or salad potatoes. Toss with cooked BROAD BEANS and roughly chopped rashers of grilled back BACON.

Cold rice

STUFFED VINE LEAVES

Buy a packet of VINE LEAVES and open them out on a flat surface. Fill with a mixture of cold RICE mixed with CURRANTS, a pinch of GROUND CINNAMON and lightly toasted FLAKED ALMONDS. Wrap up the leaves into little parcels and microwave on High for 2 minutes until they are heated through. Serve hot with freshly ground black pepper and a wedge of LEMON.

SPANISH RICE SALAD

Boil or steam some FRENCH BEANS and PEAS until just tender. Drain. Dice half a RED PEPPER. Prepare 2–3 oz/50–75g North Atlantic PRAWNS, and/or some MUSSELS. Toss the prawns and vegetables with the rice in a dressing made with a good proportion of olive oil, with added crushed GARLIC (optional).

CHEESE RICE SALAD

Prepare a selection of summer salad vegetables such as TOMATOES, CUCUMBER, SPRING ONIONS, garden PEAS and thinly sliced COURGETTES and toss them into the left-over rice with the juice of half a LEMON and freshly chopped MINT leaves. Add cubes of a mild cheese, which goes better with this type of salad than a mature cheese. For example, Tomme de Camargue (a fresh herb-flavoured sheep's-milk cheese), or a full-fat firm cheese such as Doux de Montagne, or the ubiquitous Edam or mature Gouda . . .

GREEN PEPPER GRATIN

Make a *roux* by stirring a scant tablespoonful of plain FLOUR and the same of olive oil in a saucepan over a low heat for 2 minutes, then slowly add ⅓ pint/180ml VEGETABLE STOCK and continue to stir until the sauce thickens. Keep it warm. Place a GREEN PEPPER under a hot grill and turn from time to time for about 5 minutes. Stir 2 oz/50g grated GRUYÈRE CHEESE and 4–5 oz/100–150g cooked BROWN RICE into the sauce and leave on one side. Remove the stalk, seeds and charred skin from the pepper and chop the flesh roughly. Stir into the sauce mixture. Lastly add a tablespoonful of freshly chopped PARSLEY and transfer to an individual heatproof serving dish. Sprinkle with 1 oz/25g more grated cheese and put under a hot grill until the cheese melts.

Cold chicken

LIME PICKLE CHICKEN

Mix a small pot of thick NATURAL YOGHURT with two tablespoons of LIME PICKLE, one tablespoonful of MAYONNAISE and half a teaspoonful of GARAM MASALA. Shred the cold CHICKEN and mix with the sauce. Serve with POPPODUMS, which can be quickly prepared by microwaving on High for 2 minutes (or otherwise prepared according to the manufacturer's instructions) and MANGO CHUTNEY.

Cold pasta

PASTA SALAD

Cold pasta shells and twists make a great excuse for a pasta salad. Mix equal quantities of cold PASTA with cold cooked CHICKPEAS (always a useful store-cupboard standby) and a couple of tablespoons of HUMMUS. Serve with a contrasting 'fresh' salad if possible. Root vegetables are more likely to be on hand at short notice, so try a dish of grated CARROT and grated BEETROOT tossed in a lemony VINAIGRETTE dressing.

Cold turkey

CHRISTMAS SANDWICHES

I don't get fed up with cold turkey at Christmas (probably because I buy a smaller bird and invite lots of friends for lunch!) but even if I did have lots of left-over turkey I am sure it would run out before I became tired of cold turkey sandwiches. They have to be made with WHOLEMEAL BREAD and the turkey must not be dry. Spread the bread with Flora or some such equivalent, and arrange slices of cold TURKEY topped with finely chopped SPRING ONIONS, MAYONNAISE and CRANBERRY SAUCE. That's it.

Index

aïoli 75, 98
allspice 60, 62, 120
almonds:
  fried almonds and spinach 109
  in other recipes 57, 74, 106, 122
anchovies:
  with ravioli 68
  in Salade Niçoise 76
  in sandwiches 99
  walnut and anchovy pâté 34
  in other recipes 69, 96
apples:
  granola layer 121
  guava and apple strudel 42, 120
  with liver 61
  in puddings 114, 116
  salad 50
apricots
  with brown-bread ice cream 117
  and duck 53
  in puddings 115, 121
artichokes:
  in pizzas 96
  in salads 82, 95
asparagus 92, 99
aubergines:
  chickpeas and aubergines 107
  salads 73, 80, 81-2
  in other recipes 31, 48
avocados: salads 72, 77, 78, 83, 87

bacon:
  and dates 97
  in fish recipes 44-5, 46, 48
  pasta and bacon soup 103
  with quail 53
  with rigatoni 66
  sandwiches and salads 30, 87, 99
bacon cures 30
bagels 31
bananas:
  banana fruit cocktail 38
  peanut butter and banana
    sandwich 99
  in salad 74
basil 67, 69, 73, 75, 76, 82
batavia 75, 76, 81, 82; see also salads
bay leaves 42

beans:
  fibre content 19
  beansprouts 63-4, 77
  broad 35, 42, 79, 126
  fava 81
  (French) butter 75, 110, 127
  green 48, 72, 84-5, 88-9, 106
  kidney 110
  in salads 72, 75, 76, 79, 81, 84-5,
    88-9, 110, 126
beef:
  beefburgers 60-1
  boeuf en croûte 63
  kebabs 61-2
  sandwich 99
  stir-fry 63-4
  tournedos 63
  Turkish pizza 62
beetroot: in salads 72, 76, 128
biscuits
content 19
blackcurrants 115, 116
borek 109-10
bread:
  fibre content 19
  varieties: ciabatta (Italian) 33, 35,
    82; focaccia 95, 96; garlic 47;
    Granary 50; olive oil 94; pan
    bagnat 98; pitta 56, 81;
    poîlane 31-2, 97, 99;
    pumpernickel 94, 99; rye 30, 32,
    97, 99; walnut 85; wholemeal 19,
    30, 32, 40, 87, 122, 128
broccoli:
  with ravioli 68
  yoghurt dip 92
buckwheat crêpes 119
bulgur 62, 80, 108
butter: fat content 17, 18
buttermilk 38, 102

cabbage 54, 57, 63
cakes: content 17, 19
calories 18, 31, 93
capers 69, 76, 96
carbohydrates 16, 18, 20
carbonara: pepper and mushroom 68
cardamoms 46

Caribbean chowder 104
carrots:
    in salads 74, 86, 92, 108, 128
    in soup 49, 102, 104
    in other recipes 42, 48, 54, 61, 63
cauliflower:
    salsify, cauliflower and cheese salad
        81
    with spiced eggs 106
celery:
    cooked 49, 50, 55, 67, 103
    in salads 74, 76, 86, 93
cereals, breakfast 19, 121
cheese:
    fat content 17
    in microwave oven 36
    chèvre on toast 31–2
    green pepper gratin 127
    onion and cheese pancakes 108
    oysters mornay 49
    ricotta and spinach parcels 32
    Stilton and walnut pâté 35
    with fish 33, 34, 41, 49, 68–9
    in pasta dishes 66–7, 68–9
    in puddings 117, 122
    in salads 50, 73, 80, 81, 82, 85, 86,
        87, 127
    for snack meals 31–2, 90, 93, 94,
        95, 96, 97, 99
    varieties: bleu d'Auvergne 80;
        Boursin 99; Brie 36, 93;
        Cambozola 97, 99;
        Camembert 36, 85, 93;
        Cheddar 108; cottage 33;
        cream 31, 93; curd 31, 34, 117;
        Dolcelatte 96; Edam 93, 99, 127;
        feta 73, 81; *fromage frais* 41,
        68–9; goat's 31–2, 78, 86, 93;
        Gouda 127; Gruyère 49, 127,
        108; Mozzarella 73, 82, 96;
        Parmesan 66, 67, 87, 92, 96;
        quark 31, 33, 34, 41, 97;
        Ricotta 32, 67, 110, 122;
        Stilton 35, 81, 99
cherries:
    fresh cherry yoghurt 116
    in fruit kebabs 115
chervil 48

chèvre on toast 31–2
chicken
    burgers 61
    chicken tikka 87, 88
    cheese and chicken salad 78
    green chicken soup 103
    honey and lime chicken thighs 56–7
    kebabs 56
    lime pickle chicken 128
    liver pâté 34
    liver pilau 64
    liver salads 84, 88–9
    smoked with olive bread 94
    smoked sandwich 99
    tandoori 55
chickpeas
    and aubergine 107
    in other recipes 33, 107, 128
chicory 75, 81, 86
chillies:
    chilli prawns 46
    in salad 89
    in soups 49, 104
    in other recipes 55, 61, 62, 107, 108
Chinese dishes 19, 32, 62
chives 31, 33, 40, 48, 94, 102, 111
chops: Chinese 62
cider: in recipes 60, 119
cinnamon 57, 62, 67, 106, 108, 114,
    116, 118, 120, 121, 126
clams with spaghetti 66–7
cloves 62, 67, 114, 116, 120
cod
    fast-food pie 43
    kebabs 44–5
    smoked roe 40, 99–100
coley: Caribbean chowder 104
convenience foods 13–14
coriander 33, 46, 62, 86, 88, 104, 107,
    108, 126
courgettes:
    courgette and prawn mayonnaise 78
    in other recipes 44, 47, 54, 56, 107
crab:
    aïoli and crab 98
    with grapefruit salad 74
cream 17, 48, 53, 56, 68, 102, 114
crème fraîche 48, 53, 102, 114

crêpes suzette 119
croutons 87
cucumbers:
  in salads 74, 80, 81, 86, 87, 92, 127
  sauce 41
  walnut and c. soup 102
cumin 55, 62, 81, 87, 88, 106, 107, 126
currants 57, 64, 108, 110, 126
curries:
  beefburgers (with curry spices) 61
  chilli prawns 46
  monkfish masala 42–3
  Tandoori chicken 55
  Tikka drumsticks 88

dates:
  with bacon 97
  in fruit kebab 115
dill 40, 69, 78
dried fruit *petits-fours* 122
drinks 38
duck 52
  with apricots 53
  Barbary breast salad 89
  smoked with lentils 85
Dumas, Alexandre 9

eel, smoked: fish platter 40
eggs:
  quail 42, 106, 108
  in salads 76, 78, 84, 98
  sandwiches 99
  Scotch 86, 106
  scrambled with smoked salmon 94
  shirred with salmon 33
  spiced with cauliflower 106
  in other recipes 34, 43, 48, 62, 63, 68, 92, 98, 103, 108, 119
  see also omelettes
equipment 22–3
escarole *see* batavia *and* salads

fagioli con tonno 76
fats 17, 88, 92
fibre 19–20
figs:
  cream and fig sandwich 99

  in fruit-salad tartlets 115
fish
  bacon and fish kebabs 44–5
  chowder 104
  fast-food pie 43
  oils 17
  salads 50, 74–5
  smoked fish platter 40
  stock 42, 44, 47, 49, 77, 104
fishcakes: salmon 40
focaccia 95, 96
food poisoning 34, 84, 89
fruit salads 114–15

game calendar 52
gammon with grapes 60
garam masala 42, 55, 58, 124
garlic:
  in delicatessen recipes 31, 32, 33, 34, 98
  with fish 44, 45, 46, 47, 49, 98
  with game 53, 55
  with meat 61, 63
  with pasta dishes 66, 68, 69, 95, 103
  in salads 76, 79, 80, 81, 84, 87, 88, 92, 127
  in soups 103, 104
  in vegetarian recipes 108, 109, 110
gelatine 123
Gelozone 123
ginger 47, 49, 55, 63, 88, 89, 104, 106
goose:
  smoked goose salad 79
  smoked with lentils 85
gooseberries:
  Chinese 115
  gooseberry fool 116–17
granola layer 121
grapefruit:
  pink grapefruit passion juice 38
  in salads 74, 77–8
grapes:
  in fruit kebab 115
  with gammon 60
  in salads 50, 84
grouse: season 52
guava and apple strudel 42, 120
guinea fowl 52

haddock: kebabs 44–6
halibut on tomato sauce 41
ham:
    with broad beans 35
    with fruit 97, 98
    with olive bread 94
    Parma parcels 33
    in salads 82
    sandwich 99
hare: season 52
hazelnuts and hazelnut dressing 72, 77, 84, 85, 86
healthy diet 16
herring:
    pickled herring sandwich 99
    Swedish sild salad 76
honey:
    with gammon 60
    and lime chicken thighs 56–7
    in lime pressé 38
    in puddings 115
hummus 33, 128

ice-cream 116, 117
icing 120
Indian dishes 19, 36, 42–3, 46, 55, 61, 62, 88

juniper berries 54

kebabs:
    bacon and fish 44–5
    chicken 56
    fruit 115
    ground meat 61–2
    lamb 61
kibbeh 108
kidneys in sherry 60

lamb:
    burgers 61
    Chinese chops 62
    kebabs 61–2
    meatballs with tagliatelle 67–8
    Turkish pizza 62
langoustine and grapefruit salad 77–8
leeks 43–4, 48, 54, 102
left-overs 125

lemon dressing 74
lentils:
    carrot and lentil soup 104
    with chorizo 35
    Continental lentil salad 84
    with mussels 45–6
    nut rissoles 107
    with smoked duck 85
lettuce:
    bacon and lettuce sandwich 30
    see also salads
limes:
    drinks 38
    honey and lime chicken thighs 56–7
    lime pickle chicken 128
liver:
    chicken pâté 34
    chicken pilau 64
    chicken salads 84, 88–9
    one-pot 61

macaroni and bacon soup 103
mace 33, 34
mackerel, smoked:
    and apple salad 50
    fish platter 40
    pâté 33
    in stuffed tomatoes 94
mangoes:
    in fruit puddings 115, 117
    lime and mango drink 38
maple syrup with creamy orange 118
margarine: content 17, 18
marinades 56, 57, 62, 63–4, 88
marjoram 45, 78
mayonnaise: courgette and prawn 78
meat, organic 7, 10, 59
melons:
    in fruit kebab 115
    with ham 33
    Italian melon salad 82
    melon zinger 38
meringue Melba 116
microwave ovens 13–14, 21–2, 36, 94
mince:
    beefburgers 60–1
    kebabs 61–2
    with tagliatelle 67–8

monkfish:
  kebabs 44
  masala 42–3
  Provençal 45
moules marinière 47
mushrooms:
  pepper and mushroom carbonara
  68
  salads 79–80, 84–5
  in other recipes 43, 54, 56, 63, 96,
  110
mussels:
  fish platter 40
  with lentils 45–6
  moules marinière 47
  with rice salad 127
mustard:
  sauce 40
  seeds 55, 88, 106, 107, 126

noodles, egg 49
nut rissoles 107
nutmeg 57, 108, 114, 116

oils 17, 18
okra 104
olives 96
  olive spread 99
  in other dishes 73, 76, 79, 81, 98,
  109
omelettes:
  aux truffes 32–3
  tortilla 109
oranges:
  caramelized 117
  creamy orange with maple syrup 118
  orange dressing 88
  poussin with orange stuffing 55
  in other recipes 46, 54, 55, 62, 63,
  89, 118
oregano 45, 78
oysters:
  à l'Américaine 49
  brochettes 48
  grilled 48
  mornay 49
  sauce 63

pain poîlane 31–2, 97, 99
pan bagnat 98
pancakes:
  buckwheat crêpes 119
  cheese and onion 108
  crêpes suzette 119
  fruity 118–19
paprika 53, 75, 104
partridge: season 52
passion fruit: pink grapefruit passion
  fruit juice 38
pasta 66–9
  pasta *provençale* 69
  salad 128
pastrami on rye 30
pastries:
  content 17, 19
  stuffed (*borek*) 109–10
pastry:
  filo 32, 42, 93, 109–10, 115, 120
  puff 43, 63
pâté:
  chicken liver 34
  olive 54
  smoked mackerel 33
  smoked salmon 34, 77
  stilton and walnut 35
  walnut and anchovy 34
pawpaws:
  pawpaw salad 115
  with Parma ham 98
peaches:
  cheese and peach parcels 93
  in fruit salads 114, 115
  grilled 117
  salads 77, 82
peanut butter and banana sandwich 99
pears:
  cheese and pear salads 80
  ham and pear sandwich 99
  in hot fruit salad 114
  with smoked trout 97
peas 42, 43, 48, 54, 63, 127
peppercorns 42, 54
peppers:
  green pepper gratin 127
  mushroom and pepper carbonara 68
  in main recipes 44, 48, 56, 63, 69

in salads 73, 74, 76, 78, 92, 98, 110, 127
in snacks and soups 92, 96, 104
petits-fours, dried fruit 122
pheasant: season 52
pies: fat content 17
pigeon 52
with cinnamon rice 57
pine kernels 32, 46, 64, 67, 110
pineapples:
in fruit kebab 115
prawn and pineapple salad 50
pizza:
dough and toppings 95–6
and focaccia bread 95
Turkish 62
plums:
with cheese and *Poîlane* 99
in fruit kebab 115
polyunsaturated fats 17, 18, 30
poppodums 36, 128
pork:
kebabs 61–2
stuffing 54
potatoes:
cornichon (la Ratte) 41, 45
Indian 126
instant 43
monkfish provençal with
potatoes 45
pink fir apple 41, 62
quail and turnip dauphinoise 53
rosti 111
salads 75–6, 79, 126
tortilla 109
vegetable and potatoes soup 102
poussin 52
devilled 57
with orange stuffing 55
prawns:
and aïoli 98
Caribbean chowder 104
chilli 46
Chinese prawn toast 32
courgette and prawn mayonnaise 78
creole 44
salads 50, 74, 76–7, 127
sandwiches 99

pressure cookers 21, 22, 42–3
pulses: fibre content 19
purslane 72, 85

quail 52
boned stuffed 54
eggs 42, 106, 108
with potato and turnip
dauphinoise 53
smoked with olive bread 94
on toast 53–4
quark *see* cheese

rabbit: season 52
radicchio 72, 74, 80, 84, 87, 92
raisins 50, 114, 120
raspberries 115, 116
ratatouille 48
ravioli with broccoli 68
redcurrants 115, 118
red oak leaf (feuille de chêne) 72, 75, 77, 79, 85
red pepper soup 104
rhubarb:
fruit brûlée 116
strawberry and rhubarb
compote 118
rice:
cooking 42, 43
with fish dishes 43–4, 45, 46, 47, 48
with game dishes 53, 54, 55, 56, 57
with meat dishes 60, 64
salads 110, 126–7
ricotta and spinach parcels 32
rigatoni with bacon 66
rocket 72, 85, 97
rosemary 44
rosti 111
roux 48, 49, 127

saffron 43, 88
sage 61
salads:
fish 50, 74–8
green 72
meat 35, 78–9
miscellaneous 73–4, 79–82, 110, 127

Salads – *cont.*
  tièdes (warm) 84–89
  wild 42, 72
Sally Lunn 121
salmon:
  fresh salmon fishcakes 40
  fresh salmon salad 77
  fresh salmon steaks on cucumber
   sauce 41
  fresh salmon tartlets 42
  smoked salmon on bagels 31
  smoked salmon with dill 68–9
  smoked salmon fish platter 40
  smoked salmon pâté 34
  smoked salmon salad 75, 77
  smoked salmon sandwich 99
  smoked salmon with scrambled
   eggs 94
  smoked salmon with shirred eggs 33
salsify, cauliflower and cheese salad 81
salt 16
sandwiches:
  bacon, lettuce and tomato 30
  open 99
  pan bagnat 98
  sweet toasted 122
  turkey 128
sauces:
  horseradish 30, 40
  oyster 63, 79
  for ravioli 68
  soy 43, 63, 77, 79, 103, 109
  tomato 41, 86–7
  white wine 49
sausage: chorizo 35
scallops:
  brochettes 48
  with vegetables 48
  with wild rice 43–4
scones with brandy butter 122
sesame seeds 32
setting agents 123
shallots 47, 48, 49, 60, 66, 67
sherry: in recipes 60, 79
  vinegar: in recipes 53, 57
single-eater syndrome 15
skate, steamed 47
slimming 20

snipe: season 52
soups:
  bacon and pasta 103
  Caribbean chowder 104
  carrot and lentil 104
  cucumber and walnut 102
  green chicken 103
  hot prawn 49
  potato and raw vegetable 102–3
  red pepper 104
  watercress 102
spaghetti:
  with spinach and nuts 67
  vongole 66–7
spinach:
  in *borek* 109
  fried almonds and spinach 109
  ricotta and spinach 32
  salads 72, 87
  spaghetti with spinach and nuts 67
spring onions 75, 79, 80, 89, 103, 110,
  127, 128
squid, stuffed 46–7
steak: beefburgers 60–1
stock:
  in fish recipes 42, 44, 47, 48, 49, 77
  in game recipes 54, 57
  in meat recipes 60
  for soup 102, 103, 104
  in vegetarian recipes 35, 106, 127
strawberries:
  in fruit salads 115
  rhubarb and strawberry
   compôte 118
  fool 116
  shortcake 116
  sling 38
strudel, apple and guava 42, 120
strudel leaves *see* pastry, filo
stuffing 46–7, 54, 55
sugar 16, 18–19, 20
sugar loaf (*pain de sucre*) 72
sweet and sour dressing 77
sweetcorn 43, 54, 63, 104
swordfish: braised 45

taboulleh 80
tagliatelle and meatballs 67–8

tagliolini 67
tahini 33
tamari 49
taramosalata 40, 99
tarragon 31
tayberries: in fruit kebab 115
thyme 44, 45, 62
Tikka recipes 87, 88
tofu 110
tomatoes:
  bacon sandwich 30
  sauce 41, 86–7
  soup 104
  stuffed 94
  in fish recipes 41, 44, 45, 46–7, 49
  in game recipes 55, 57
  in meat recipes 61, 62
  in misc. recipes 107, 127
  in pasta recipes 67, 68, 69, 96
  in salads 73, 75, 76, 78, 81, 82, 84, 98, 127
tortelloni with ricotta cheese 67
tortilla 109
trifle, instant 121
trout
  fresh trout en croûte 43
  smoked 97
  smoked trout vol-au-vents 41
truffle omelette 32–3
tuna:
  braised 45
  salads 75, 76
  smoked roe 40
  in stuffed tomatoes 94
turkey:
  escalopes 56
  sandwiches 128
Turkish dishes 31, 62, 80, 81, 108, 109
turmeric 46, 88, 106
turnips 53, 110

vegetarian dishes 86, 106–11
venison 52
  medallion of 54
  with olive bread 94
vermicelli 67
vine leaves, stuffed 126
vol-au-vents: smoked trout 41

walnuts:
  cucumber and walnut soup 102
  dressing 86
  pâté 34
  in petits-fours 122
  salads and sandwiches 75, 85, 99
  in Scotch eggs 106
watercress:
  in salads 54, 72, 78, 86, 87, 93, 97
  soups 102, 103
wheat, cracked *see* bulgur
white sauce 49
wine 36
  in recipes 42, 47, 49, 56, 61, 66–7
woodcock: season 52

yoghurt:
  in cooked dishes 41, 55, 61, 106
  dip 92, 128
  in drinks 38
  in puddings 114, 116, 118, 120, 121
  in salads 50, 74, 76–7, 81, 88
  in soup 102

FOOD AND COOKING IN PENGUIN

The Fratelli Camisa Cookery Book   Elizabeth Camisa

From antipasti to zabaglione, from the origins of gorgonzola to the storage of salami, an indispensable guide to real Italian home cooking from Elizabeth Camisa of the famous Fratelli Camisa delicatessen in Soho's Berwick Street.

A Table in Tuscany   Leslie Forbes

With authentic recipes and beautiful illustrations, artist and cook Leslie Forbes evokes the rich flavour of Tuscany, from its Renaissance palaces to its robust red Chianti. More than a cookery book and more than mere travel writing, *A Table in Tuscany* is a culinary odyssey.

The Food and Cooking of Eastern Europe   Lesley Chamberlain

Diverse, appetizing and often surprisingly sophisticated, the cuisine of Eastern Europe goes far beyond the goulash and beetroot soup familiar to the West. From the refreshing fruit soups of Hungary to the fish dishes of Dalmatia, this is a fascinating tour of Eastern gastronomy.

Out to Lunch   Paul Levy

Gloriously entertaining essays from Britain's best-known writer on food and drink as he eats out around the world. Whether you want to know more about truffle-hunting, cheeses, aphrodisiacs or the great American sandwich, or whether people actually do eat dogs in Macao, all the answers are here.

The Penguin Book of Jams, Pickles and Chutneys   David and Rose Mabey

'An excellent book; practical, personal and suggestive, every recipe's clearly the result of real experience and written with great charm' – *The Times*

More Easy Cooking for One or Two   Louise Davies

This charming book, full of ideas and easy recipes, offers even the novice cook good wholesome food with the minimum of effort.

FOOD AND COOKING IN PENGUIN

The Philosopher in the Kitchen Jean-Anthelme Brillat-Savarin

In this utterly unprecedented collection of recipes, experiences, reflections, history and philosophy, gastronomy is raised to the level of an art. Witty, shrewd and anecdotal, it contains both some superb recipes for food and some highly satisfying observations on life.

The Food and Cooking of Russia Lesley Chamberlain

'The first really good book on this fascinating subject. I read it from cover to cover as one would a novel' – Paul Levy. 'A fine book … recipes to suit all tastes and moods – from the refined traditions of the nineteenth-century nobility to Ukrainian peasant dishes and spicy creations from Central Asia' – Alan Davidson

Scottish Regional Recipes Catherine Brown

Bridal cake from Orkney, chicken stovies from the Highlands, Morayshire apples from the north-east … Born out of local conditions and shaped by ingenuity and care throughout the centuries, these robust and satisfying recipes have stood the test of time.

English Bread and Yeast Cookery Elizabeth David

'Here is a real book, written with authority and enthusiasm – a collection of history, investigation, comment, recipes' – Jane Grigson. 'Quite outstanding … erudite without losing the common touch – or the interest of the reader' – *Spectator*

Josceline Dimbleby's Book of Puddings, Desserts and Savouries

'Full of the most delicious and novel ideas for every type of pudding' – *The Lady*

The Cookery of England Elisabeth Ayrton

Her fascinating and beautifully compiled history and recipe book of English cooking from the fifteenth century to the present day is 'a lovely book, which could restore pride to our English kitchens' – *The Times Literary Supplement*

FOR THE BEST IN PAPERBACKS, LOOK FOR THE 🐧

FROM THE PENGUIN COOKERY LIBRARY

The Best of Eliza Acton   Selected and Edited by Elizabeth Ray
With an Introduction by Elizabeth David

First published in 1845, Eliza Acton's *Modern Cookery for Private Families*, of which this is a selection, is a true classic which everyone interested in cookery will treasure.

Easy to Entertain   Patricia Lousada

Easy to Entertain hands you the magic key to entertaining without days of panic or last minute butterflies. The magic lies in cooking each course ahead, so that you can enjoy yourself along with your guests.

French Provincial Cooking   Elizabeth David

'It is difficult to think of any home that can do without Elizabeth David's *French Provincial Cooking* ... One could cook for a lifetime on the book alone' – *Observer*

The National Trust Book of Traditional Puddings   Sara Paston-Williams

'My favourite cookbook of the year. Engagingly written ... this manages to be both scholarly and practical, elegant without pretension' – *Sunday Times*

The New Book of Middle Eastern Food   Claudia Roden

'This is one of those rare cookery books that is a work of cultural anthropology and Mrs Roden's standards of scholarship are so high as to ensure that it has permanent value' – Paul Levy in the *Observer*

Charcuterie and French Pork Cookery   Jane Grigson

'Fully comprehensive ... a detailed and enlightening insight into the preparation and cooking of pork. Altogether a unique book' – *Wine and Food*. 'The research is detailed, the recounting lively, the information fascinating' – *The Times*

FOOD AND COOKING IN PENGUIN

Traditional Jamaican Cookery Norma Benghiat

Reflecting Arawak, Spanish, African, Jewish, English, French, East Indian and Chinese influences, the exciting recipes in this definitive book range from the lavish eating of the old plantocracy to imaginative and ingenious slave and peasant dishes.

Cooking in a Bedsit Katharine Whitehorn

Practical and light-hearted, the perfect book for those cooking in limited space, with little time and less money – problems that can easily be surmounted with imagination, common sense and a great deal of newspaper. 'All parents with bedsitter children should send them a copy' – *Observer*

The Beginner's Cookery Book Betty Falk

Revised and updated, this book is for aspiring cooks of all ages who want to make appetizing and interesting meals without too much fuss. With an emphasis on healthy eating, this is the ideal starting point for would-be cooks.

Jane Grigson's Fruit Book

Fruit is colourful, refreshing and life-enhancing; this book shows how it can also be absolutely delicious in meringues or compotes, soups or pies.

Fast Food for Vegetarians Janette Marshall

Packed with ideas for healthy, delicious dishes from Caribbean vegetables to rose-water baklava, this stimulating book proves that fast food does not have to mean junk food.

Malaysian Cookery Rafi Fernandez

A step-by-step guide to the intoxicating, fragrant, colourful cuisine of Malaysia: the origins of its three distinct culinary strands, traditional cooking techniques and customs, where to buy the more exotic ingredients – and a mouthwatering selection of recipes.